VISTAS

An Interactive Course in English

2

Project Director   H. Douglas Brown

Senior Writers
Tony Silva
Sharon Seymour
Pamela Polos

Contributing Writers
Amelia Kreitzer
Bradley Reed
Nancy Schaefer
Jean Svacina
Kathy Varchetto

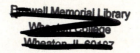

Prentice Hall Regents
Englewood Cliffs, New Jersey 07632

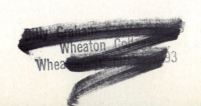

Library of Congress Cataloging-in-Publication Data

Brown, H. Douglas, 1941–
  Vistas: an interactive course in English / H. Douglas Brown.
  p.   cm.

  ISBN 0-13-650334-9 (student book: v. 2)
  1. English language—Textbooks for foreign speakers.   I.
Title.
PE1128.B725 1991
428.2′4—dc20   90-44440
                                       CIP

Publisher: Tina B. Carver
Manager of Product Development: Mary Vaughn
Senior Editor: Larry Anger
Development Editor: Louisa B. Hellegers
Managing Editor, Production: Sylvia Moore
Senior Production Editor: Janet S. Johnston
Production Editor: Shirley Hinkamp
Audio Editor: Stephanie Karras
Design Director: Janet Schmid
Design Coordinator: Christine Wolf
Pre-Press Buyer: Ray Keating
Manufacturing Buyer: Lori Bulwin
Scheduler: Leslie Coward
Interior and Cover Designer: Suzanne Bennett

Illustrators: Glenn Davis, Don Martinetti
Cover Photo: Donald C. Johnson/The Stock Market
Page Layout: Claudia Durrell Design
Audio Production: Phyllis Dolgin

Photo Credits

page 22: Laimute E. Druskis
    70: New York views—*NY Convention & Visitors Bureau*
    71: Big Ben—*British Information Services*
           Colosseum—*Italian Government Travel Office*
           Forbidden City—*Morris Simoncelli/Japan Airlines*
           Meiji Temple—*Michal Heron*
           Pyramid of the Sun—*Robin W. Winks*
  107: Miami views—*Miami Convention & Visitors Bureau*
  118: Swimming—*Laimute E. Druskis*
           Garbage—*Tony Freeman/PhotoEdit*
           Skiing—*Swiss National Tourist Office*
           Painting—*Sonya Jacobs/The Stock Market*

© 1992 by Prentice-Hall, Inc.
A Simon & Schuster Company
Englewood Cliffs, New Jersey 07632

Printed in the United States of America

10   9   8   7   6   5   4   3

ISBN 0-13-650334-9

Prentice-Hall International (UK) Limited, *London*
Prentice-Hall of Australia Pty. Limited, *Sydney*
Prentice-Hall Canada Inc., *Toronto*
Prentice-Hall Hispanoamericana, S.A., *Mexico*
Prentice-Hall of India Private Limited, *New Delhi*
Prentice-Hall of Japan, Inc., *Tokyo*
Simon & Schuster Asia Pte. Ltd., *Singapore*
Editora Prentice-Hall do Brasil, Ltda., *Rio de Janeiro*

Field Testers and Reviewers

Prentice Hall Regents would like to thank the following field
testers and reviewers of *Vistas*, whose insights and suggestions
helped to shape the content and format of the series: Julia
Berenguer de Soltice, Valencia, Spain; Walther Bolzmann,
Coordinator of Evaluation, *TRANSLEX*, Lima, Peru; Mary Ann
Corley, ESOL Outreach Advisor, Adult Basic Education,
Baltimore County Public School, Towson, Maryland; Barbara
Goodwin, *SCS Institute*, New York, New York; Madeline
Hudders, *University of Puerto Rico*, San Juan, Puerto Rico;
Gloria Kismadi, Director of Courses, *Limbaga Amerika*,
Jakarta, Indonesia; Walter Lockhart, *Lockhart Group*,
Pamplona, Spain; Lydia Lopez, *University of Puerto Rico*,
San Juan, Puerto Rico; Janet Nieves, *Instituto Cultural
Domenico-Americano*, Santo Domingo, Dominican Republic;
Jaime Ponce, Executive Director, *TRANSLEX*, Lima, Peru;
Martin Roman, Director, *Instituto Cultural Dominico-Americano*,
Santo Domingo, Dominican Republic; Helen Slivka, New York,
New York; Daniel Soltice, Valencia, Spain; Carmen Zapata,
University of Puerto Rico, San Juan, Puerto Rico.

CONTENTS

Topics and Skills

Parties
Work
Writing an invitation

Grammar

Review: the simple present tense vs. the present continuous tense
Some verbs that don't usually end in **-ing** (**love, know, want,** etc.)
Conjunction **that**
The simple past tense: regular verbs
   affirmative statements
   yes/no questions and short answers
Expressions of past time (**yesterday, last week,** etc.)

Communication Goals

Giving and accepting compliments
Complimenting and agreeing
Apologizing and accepting an apology
Introducing people
Offering, accepting, and declining food
Exchanging personal information
Talking about the present and the past
Giving opinions

Topics and Skills

Life in the past
History and important dates
Writing a page in a diary

Grammar

Tag questions: present tense
The simple past tense
   negative statements
   information (wh-) questions
Past tense of irregular verbs
Who as subject
Anyone, someone, and **no one**
Conjunctions **so** and **because**

Communication Goals

Guessing what happened
Finding out who did something
Talking about family and friends
Talking about famous people and events
Giving reasons
Asking for confirmation

Topics and Skills

Family
Shopping for clothes
Reading a store directory
Filling out an application for a charge account

Grammar

Who as subject and short answers (**I did.**)
One and **ones**
Information (wh-) questions with **which**
Object pronouns (**me, you, him, her, it, us, them**)
Would like to
Tag questions: simple past tense

Communication Goals

Talking about the past
Asking for and giving assistance
Identifying
Asking for confirmation
Talking about size and fit

Topics and Skills

A robbery
Bargains
Reading sale ads

Grammar

The past tense of **be**
    information (wh-) questions
    affirmative and negative statements
    yes/no questions and short answers
    tag questions
There was and **there were**
(Not) as . . . as
Adjective + **to** + verb (**easy to clean**, etc.)
Comparative of adjectives (**cheaper, more economical, better than,** etc.)

Communication Goals

Talking about the past
Describing people
Comparing
Agreeing and disagreeing
Emphasizing
Making suggestions
Talking about preferences

Topics and Skills

The body and illness
Writing a note to a teacher or boss
Reading medicine labels

Grammar

Review: the comparative of adjectives
    (not) as . . . as
The superlative of adjectives (**the newest, the most successful, the best,** etc.)
Clauses with **if** in the present

Communication Goals

Comparing
Complaining
Giving opinions
Asking for and giving advice
Making suggestions
Making a doctor's appointment
Talking about illness
Offering sympathy

Topics and Skills

Vacations and travel
Reading international travel signs
Reading arrival and departure screens
Writing a postcard

Grammar

The future with **be going to**
    affirmative and negative statements
    yes/no questions and short answers
    information (wh-) questions
The immediate past with **just**
Review: verb + **to** + verb (They **like to travel.**)

Communication Goals

Talking about the future
Talking about the present and the future
Talking about the immediate past
Giving reasons
Talking about vacations
Checking in for a flight
Asking for travel information

Topics and Skills

Chores
Applying for a job
Reading abbreviations and help wanted ads
Completing a job application form
Writing a resume

Grammar

Can
   affirmative and negative statements
   yes/no questions and short answers
   tag questions
Review: **have (has) to**
Have (has) got to
Review: conjunctions **and, but, because,** and **so**

Communication Goals

Asking for and giving personal information
Talking about ability
Asking for confirmation
Giving reasons or excuses
Inviting and refusing invitations
Making requests

Topics and Skills

Marriage
Fortunetellers and horoscopes
Getting meaning from context
Writing a note with only necessary information

Grammar

The future with **will**
   affirmative and negative statements
   yes/no questions and short answers
   information (wh-) questions
Review: conjunction **that**
The conditional with **if . . . will** (possible situations)

Communication Goals

Talking about the future
Making predictions
Talking about probability
Making promises
Talking about horoscopes

Topics and Skills

Cars and driving
Advice
Taking a written driver's license examination
Writing a letter without unnecessary information

Grammar

Should
   affirmative and negative statements
   information (wh-) questions
   yes/no questions and short answers
Must
Contrast: **can, should,** and **must**
Whose
Possessive pronouns (**mine, his, hers, ours, yours, theirs**)
Too

Communication Goals

Talking about advisability
Talking about possessions
Asking for and giving advice
Rejecting a suggestion
Talking about obligation or necessity

Topics and Skills

Childhood
A surprise party
Writing an article about a classmate or oneself

Grammar

Had to
   affirmative and negative statements
   yes/no questions and short answers
   information (wh-) questions
Could (past ability)
   affirmative and negative statements
   yes/no questions and short answers
Tag questions: future tenses (**be going to** and **will**)

Have got
    affirmative and negative statements
    yes/no questions and short answers
    who as subject
Enough
A lot (of), a little, and **a few**
So + adjective or adverb (**so early, so good,** etc.)

Communication Goals

Talking about past obligation and necessity
Talking about past and present ability
Expressing surprise and interest
Asking for confirmation
Talking about availability
Talking about quantity

THE PEOPLE IN VISTAS

Olga Delgado
housewife

Tetsuo Matsumoto
teacher

Susan Balewa
petroleum engineer

Ann Brennan's
husband, Jerry
taxi driver

Keiko Abe
secretary

Roberto Rivera
reporter

Gina's boyfriend,
Frank Russo
accountant

Pravit Soongwang
mechanic

Gina Poggi
bookkeeper

Pierre Blanc
waiter

Lynn Wang
photographer

Tony Silva
architect

Oscar Garcia
doctor

Yon Mi Lee
computer programmer

Marco Martinez
security guard

Ann Brennan
teacher

Lesson Plan

Carlos Perez
carpenter

Lucy Mendoza
nurse

What's going on?

Look at the picture. Then listen as you read the conversation.

Pravit: Hi! What's going on?

Lucy: We're getting ready for the party tomorrow.

Pravit: What party?

Lucy: Pravit, you know about the party! The English students have a party every year.

Pravit: Oh. Well, I don't like parties.

Mrs. Brennan: Oh, Pravit, parties are fun! All the students are helping. Lucy and I are decorating the cafeteria.

Lucy: Lynn and Keiko are at home. Lynn's baking a cake, and Keiko's making sandwiches.

Mrs. Brennan: Right. And Tetsuo is learning some new songs. And Tony and Roberto are cleaning the tables and chairs.

Lucy: And Yon Mi is picking up some soda at the supermarket. Everybody is doing something.

Pravit: Well, I really don't like parties. They're a lot of work.

Read the conversation on page 2 again. Are these statements True (T) or False (F)?

	T	F

1. The English students have a party every year.
2. Lucy and Mrs. Brennan don't like parties.
3. Lynn is at home because she's sick.
4. Lynn and Keiko are making food for the party.
5. Tetsuo is learning some new songs.
6. Tony and Roberto are cleaning the piano.
7. Yon Mi is picking up some soda at the supermarket.
8. Pravit loves parties.

What are the students doing right now? What do they usually do? Complete these sentences with the correct forms of the verbs in parentheses.

The students **are having** a party. They **have** a party every year.

1. Tetsuo (play) the piano at the moment. He (play) the piano every day.

2. Lucy and Mrs. Brennan (decorate) the cafeteria. They always (decorate) for the class parties.

3. Keiko is at home. She (make) sandwiches. She (make) sandwiches for every class party.

4. Lynn (bake) a cake right now. She usually (bake) an excellent cake.

5. Yon Mi is at the supermarket. She (buy) some soda. She always (buy) soda for the class parties.

6. Tony and Roberto (clean) the tables and chairs now. They always (clean) well.

First ask questions about the people in exercise 2. Listen to the examples. 🔲

> **A:** **Are** the students **having** a party?
> **B:** Yes, they are.
>
> **A:** **Do** they **have** a party every year?
> **B:** Yes, they do.

Then ask your partner questions. Use the expressions below or your own ideas.

study   play a sport   eat   practice English

> **A:** **Are you** *studying* **now?**
> **B:** Yes, I am.   (No, I'm not.)
>
> **A:** **Do you** *study* **every day?**
> **B:** Yes, I do.   (No, I don't.)

Read about Susan Balewa, a new student from Nigeria. Then discuss the questions.

Susan Balewa is from Nigeria. She is the newest student in Mrs. Brennan's English class. She has a lot of friends at school, but today she is sitting alone. She usually loves parties, but right now she isn't very happy. She is thinking about her home and her family. She wants to see her parents. She needs to talk to her brothers. She hears a song from her country and remembers that it's her sister's favorite song.

Lucy is having a good time at the party. She is dancing and talking to her friends. She sees Susan. Susan is sad and Lucy doesn't know why. Lucy thinks Susan doesn't like parties. She doesn't understand that Susan is lonely.

1. Is Susan having a good time at the party? Why?
2. What is she thinking about?
3. Is Lucy having a good time at the party? Why?
4. Does she think Susan likes parties?
5. Do you like parties? Why?
6. Do you ever feel lonely?

Some verbs don't usually end in *-ing*. Read the paragraphs about Susan again to see if you can find some of these verbs. Then complete the list of verbs.

Some verbs that don't usually end in *-ing*:

1. __love__   4. _____   7. _____
2. _____   5. _____   8. _____
3. _____   6. _____   9. _____

Choose the correct form of the verbs in parentheses.

What a great party! All the students are having a good time. Lynn (**1.** has/is having) her camera. She (**2.** takes/is taking) a lot of pictures. Pierre and Olga (**3.** dance/are dancing). They (**4.** don't know/aren't knowing) that Olga's husband (**5.** watches/is watching) them. And (**6.** do you see/are you seeing) Tony and Oscar? They (**7.** eat/are eating) because they (**8.** don't want/aren't wanting) to dance.

A man (**9.** walks/is walking) into the room. It's Pravit! He (**10.** wears/is wearing) a striped shirt and plaid pants. He always (**11.** thinks/is thinking) that he dresses well, but the other students think he (**12.** needs/is needing) glasses!

Listen to the interviews. Then complete the chart with the right nationality and occupation.

Name	Nationality	Occupation	Opinion About the Party
1. Roberto	Puerto Rican	Reporter	e. He thinks it's a wonderful party.
2. Lucy			
3. Keiko			
4. Lynn			
5. Carlos			
6. Pravit			

Now listen again and match the opinions below with the right person in the chart.

Opinions
a. He feels that all parties are a lot of work.
b. He thinks everybody is having fun.
c. She thinks that this is an excellent party.
d. She thinks the party is great.
e. He thinks it's a wonderful party.
f. She knows everybody is enjoying the party.

I'm sorry I'm late.

Look at the pictures. Then listen as you read the conversation.

Mrs. Brennan:	I'm sorry I'm late.
Keiko:	That's OK. We're glad you're here. That's a beautiful dress.
Mrs. Brennan:	Thanks. I'd like you to meet my husband, Jerry.
Keiko:	Hi. It's nice to meet you.
Mr. Brennan:	Nice to meet you, too.
Mrs. Brennan:	Is everything ready for the party?
Keiko:	Don't worry, Mrs. Brennan. Everything is fine.
Mrs. Brennan:	Did Yon Mi pick up the soda?
Keiko:	Yes, she did. She picked up the soda yesterday.
Pierre:	Hi, Mrs. Brennan. Would you like some cake? It's delicious.

Read the conversation on page 6 again. Then read the statements and answer *That's right,*
That's wrong, or *It doesn't say.*

1. Mr. and Mrs. Brennan are late for the party.
2. Keiko doesn't like Mrs. Brennan's dress.
3. Keiko doesn't like Mr. Brennan's suit.
4. Everything is ready for the party.
5. Mr. and Mrs. Brennan think that the cake is delicious.

The students did many things before the party. Complete the sentences about the students.
Use the past tense of the verbs in parentheses.

> Yon Mi **picked** up the soda yesterday.

1. Tony and Roberto (clean) the chairs and tables yesterday afternoon.
2. Oscar (wash) the glasses before the party.
3. Tetsuo (learn) some new songs last week.
4. Lucy and Mrs. Brennan (decorate) the cafeteria yesterday afternoon.
5. Pierre (invite) the other teachers two weeks ago.
6. Lynn (bake) a cake last night.
7. Carlos and Susan (fix) the stereo this morning.
8. Olga (call) a babysitter last Tuesday.

Ann Brennan helped the students with the party yesterday. What about her husband? Listen and complete the sentences with the verbs in the list.

fix   work   clean   wash
paint   rest   prepare   call

> Jerry Brennan **worked** hard yesterday morning.

1. First he _____ the car in the garage.
2. Then he _____ some bookcases in the basement.
3. Then he _____ the attic.
4. Next he _____ the clothes in the laundry room.
5. Then he _____ his mother.
6. Next he _____ lunch in the kitchen.
7. Finally, of course, he _____ in the bedroom.

Refer to exercise 3 and ask questions about Jerry. 📼

> A: **Did** Jerry **work** hard yesterday morning?
> B: **Yes, he did.**
>
> A: **Did** he **work** yesterday afternoon?
> B: **No, he didn't.**

1. fix the car yesterday morning
2. paint some chairs yesterday
3. clean the attic
4. clean the basement
5. prepare lunch yesterday
6. wash the clothes yesterday
7. call his mother yesterday afternoon
8. rest yesterday afternoon

Work with a partner. Ask and answer these questions.

> A: **Did you** *work hard last week*?
> B: **Yes, I did. (No, I didn't.)**

1. work hard last week
2. cook breakfast this morning
3. clean your house last weekend
4. learn anything new yesterday
5. listen to the radio yesterday
6. study English two years ago

Interview your classmates. Find someone who . . .

	Name of Classmate
1. worked hard yesterday.	_____
2. works hard every day.	_____
3. fixed something last week.	_____
4. cleaned his or her bedroom last weekend.	_____
5. cooked breakfast this morning.	_____
6. cooks breakfast every morning.	_____
7. washed his or her clothes last week.	_____
8. called his or her parents last week.	_____
9. watched television last night.	_____
10. studied English two years ago.	_____
11. is wearing a new shirt or blouse.	_____
12. learned something new yesterday.	_____

This is a great party.

Match the exchanges with the pictures. Then listen to the exchanges.

a. A: This is a great party.
   B: Yes, it is.

b. A: That's a beautiful dress.
   B: Thanks.

c. A: I'd like you to meet my friend, Jimmy.
   B: Hi. It's nice to meet you.
   C: Nice to meet you, too.

d. A: I'm sorry I'm late.
   B: That's OK.

e. A: Would you like some cake?
   B: Yes, please.

f. A: I'm sorry I spilled coffee on your rug.
   B: That's OK. Don't worry about it.

g. A: This cake is delicious.
   B: Thank you.

h. A: This cake is delicious.
   B: Yes, it is.

How many responses (a–n) can you find for each statement (1–8)?

1. I'm sorry I'm late.
2. I'd like you to meet my boyfriend.
3. I'm glad to meet you.
4. That's a nice tie.
5. This is a great picnic.
6. Would you like a piece of cake?
7. This cake is delicious.
8. I'm sorry I spilled coffee on your rug.

a. Don't worry about it.
b. That's OK.
c. That's all right.
d. It's nice to meet you.
e. I'm glad to meet you.
f. Nice to meet you, too.
g. Glad to meet you, too.

h. Thanks.
i. Thank you.
j. It sure is!
k. Yes, it is.
l. Yes, please.
m. No, thank you.
n. It doesn't matter.

Now practice the statements and responses.

Interview a classmate. Then report your findings to the class.

A: What's your name?
B: My name's *Keiko Abe.*
A: Where are you from?
B: I'm from *Tokyo, Japan.*
A: What do you do for a living?
B: I'm *a secretary.* (I work in *an office.*/I work for *a computer company.*)

A: What do you think about your job?
B: I feel that *it's boring because I do the same thing every day.* (I think *it's interesting.*)
A: How do you feel about English?
B: I feel/think/know (that) _____.
A: How do you feel about parties?
B: I like/don't like _____. (I feel/think (that) _____.)

Listen to the conversation. Then complete the invitation. 🔊

Find out about your classmates. Take notes.

A: **When's your birthday?**
B: **It's** *May 5. (May fifth.)*

	Classmate 1	Classmate 2	Classmate 3
1. When's your birthday?	_____	_____	_____
2. What's your address?	_____	_____	_____
3. What's your telephone number?	_____	_____	_____

Pretend you are having a party for a classmate. Write an invitation.

PLEASE COME TO A BIRTHDAY PARTY!

FOR _____

WHERE _____

WHEN _____ AT _____

R.S.V.P. _____

GRAMMAR SUMMARY

REVIEW: THE SIMPLE PRESENT TENSE VS. THE PRESENT CONTINUOUS TENSE

Tetsuo **is playing** the piano at the moment.
He usually **plays** every day.

Are you **studying** now? Yes, I **am**.
Do you **study** every day? No, I **don't**.

SOME VERBS THAT DON'T USUALLY END IN *-ING*

love	hear	know	Carlos **loves** parties.
want	remember	like	
need	see	understand	

CONJUNCTION: *THAT*

I think		it's a wonderful party.
He feels	**(that)**	all parties are a lot of work.
She knows		everybody is enjoying the party.

THE SIMPLE PAST TENSE: REGULAR VERBS

Affirmative Statements

I You He She It We They	**worked**	yesterday.

Yes/No Questions

Did	I you he she it we they	**work**	yesterday?

Short Answers

Yes,	I you he she it we they	**did.**

No,	I you he she it we they	**didn't.**

EXPRESSIONS OF PAST TIME

I worked	yesterday.
	yesterday afternoon.
	this morning.
	last week.
	last weekend.
	two weeks ago.

attic
basement
boring
camera
delicious
fun
glad
laundry room
opinion
other
parents
party
piano
plaid
rug
sandwich
striped
them

at the moment
What's going on?

VOCABULARY

VERBS

dance
decorate
dress
feel
get ready (for)
have a good time
invite
learn
pick up (=buy)
rest
see
spill
think (about)
walk

COMMUNICATION SUMMARY

GIVING AND ACCEPTING COMPLIMENTS

That's a beautiful dress.
　Thanks.
This cake is delicious.
　Thank you.

APOLOGIZING AND ACCEPTING AN APOLOGY

I'm sorry I'm late.
　That's OK. Don't worry about it.
I'm sorry I spilled coffee on your rug.
　It doesn't matter.
　That's all right.

INTRODUCING PEOPLE

I'd like you to meet my husband.
　I'm glad to meet you.
Glad to meet you, too.

EXCHANGING PERSONAL INFORMATION

What's your name?
　My name's Keiko.
Where are you from?
　Japan.
What do you do?
　I'm a secretary.
When's your birthday?
　It's August 12.
What's your address?
　1202 Marine Drive.
What's your telephone number?
　555–8974.

TALKING ABOUT THE PRESENT

The students are having a party.
They have a party every year.
Are you studying now?
　Yes, I am.
Do you study every day?
　No, I don't.

GIVING OPINIONS

What do you think about your job?
　I think that it's interesting.
How do you feel about parties?
　I feel they are a lot of fun.

COMPLIMENTING AND AGREEING

This is a great party.
　It sure is!
This cake is delicious.
　Yes, it is.

OFFERING, ACCEPTING, AND DECLINING FOOD

Would you like some cake?
　Yes, please.
　No, thank you.

TALKING ABOUT THE PAST

Jerry worked hard yesterday.
Did you learn anything new yesterday?
　Yes, I did.
　No, I didn't.

The cafeteria's a mess, isn't it?

Look at the picture. Then listen as you read the conversation. 📼

Janitor 1: Wow! The cafeteria's a mess, isn't it?

Janitor 2: Yes, it is. What happened?

Janitor 1: I guess the students didn't clean the cafeteria after the party last night, and no one closed the window.

Janitor 2: And no one turned off the lights either. Did the party end late?

Janitor 1: Yeah. It ended around midnight.

Janitor 2: Well, let's get started.

Are these statements True (T) or False (F)? Look at the picture on page 14 and decide.

	T	F

1. No one closed the windows after the party.
2. Someone removed the decorations.
3. No one cleaned the tables.
4. Someone picked up the garbage.
5. Someone turned off the lights.
6. No one erased the board.
7. No one returned the extra chairs.
8. Someone cleaned the floor.

The students didn't clean the cafeteria after the party. What happened? Look at the list of THINGS TO DO AFTER THE PARTY and practice the conversation.

A: **Wow! The cafeteria's a mess, isn't it?**
B: **Yes, it is. What happened?**
A: **I guess** *Oscar didn't close the windows.*

THINGS TO DO AFTER THE PARTY

1. close the windows – Oscar
2. erase the board – Keiko
3. clean the tables – Lucy and Gina
4. return the extra chairs – Pierre and Marco
5. remove the decorations – Lynn
6. pick up the garbage – Roberto
7. wash the dishes – Pravit
8. clean the floor – Carlos

Make statements and ask for confirmation. Your partner will agree with you.
Look at the examples below. 📼

A: The cafeteria's a mess, **isn't** it?
B: Yes, it is.

A: The floor **isn't** very clean, **is** it?
B: No, it isn't.

A: The tables **are** pretty dirty, **aren't** they?
B: Yes, they are.

A: The students **aren't** cleaning now, **are** they?
B: No, they aren't.

A: The students **like** parties, **don't** they?
B: Yes, they do.

A: They **don't** like to clean after their parties, **do** they?
B: No, they don't.

A: Mrs. Brennan **likes** parties too, **doesn't** she?
B: Yes, she does.

A: But she **doesn't** like to clean either, **does** she?
B: No, she doesn't.

1. A: We're learning English now, _____?
   B: _____.

2. A: English isn't easy, _____?
   B: _____.

3. A: Our classmates are nice, _____?
   B: _____.

4. A: You like English, _____?
   B: _____.

5. A: The teacher teaches well, _____?
   B: _____.

6. A: We don't speak English very well, _____?
   B: _____.

7. A: The teacher doesn't like lazy students, _____?
   B: _____.

8. A: We work hard in class, _____?
   B: _____.

Work with a group. Look at the pictures and complete the statements with the verbs in parentheses. Then listen and check your answers. 📼

Tony **didn't study** Saturday night.

Pierre **worked** at the restaurant yesterday.

1. Pravit (fix) _____ the car this morning.

2. Gina (dance) _____ a lot last night.

3. Carlos (enjoy) _____ the movie last week.

4. Keiko and Lynn (shop) _____ for food last weekend.

5. Susan (miss) _____ the bus two days ago.

6. Mrs. Brennan (close) _____ the window before class on Friday.

7. Oscar (spill) _____ his drink at the class party.

8. Olga and Hector (paint) _____ their living room yesterday.

A woman is talking to her family. Listen to the conversation. Which things did the woman's family do? Answer Yes or No.

	Yes	No
1. Did anyone fix the car?		
2. Did anyone fix the refrigerator?		
3. Did anyone clean the bathroom?		
4. Did anyone clean the kitchen?		
5. Did anyone pick up the mess in the living room?		
6. Did anyone pick up the mess in the dining room?		
7. Did anyone talk to Grandma?		
8. Did anyone talk to Grandpa?		
9. Did anyone shop for lunch?		
10. Did anyone shop for dinner?		

Look at the answers in exercise 5 and practice the conversation.

A: **Did anyone** *fix the car*?

B: **Someone** *fixed the car*, **but no one** *fixed the refrigerator*.

Work with a group. First, make a list of questions for the class. After you make your list, ask the class your questions and count the students who raise their hands.

Sample Questions	Number of Students
1. Did anyone work yesterday?	_____
2. Did anyone cook dinner last night?	_____
3. Did anyone in this class study English before?	_____
4. Did anyone visit a foreign country last year?	_____
5. Did anyone go to the zoo last week?	_____

Now report the information to the class like this:

Number of Students	
1	One student worked yesterday.
3	Three students cooked dinner last night.
All	Everybody in this class studied English before.
0	No one visited a foreign country last year.

LESSON 2

My grandparents

Look at the pictures from Gina's photo album. Then listen as you read the paragraphs.

My grandmother grew up in a small town. Her house didn't have electricity, and her family didn't have a telephone. She went to school far from her home. Her parents didn't have a car so she had to walk. After school she took care of her brothers and sisters.

My grandfather grew up in the next town. My grandmother met my grandfather at a dance in 1920. One year later, they got married. My grandparents bought a farm and built a big house for their family. They had six children. My grandparents didn't have a lot of money, but they gave their children a lot of love. They had a good life.

The past tense of the verbs in the paragraphs on page 19 are irregular. Match the past tense with the present tense.

PRESENT	PAST
1. grow (up)	a. had
2. have/has (to)	b. got
3. go	c. grew
4. take (care of)	d. took
5. meet	e. built
6. get (married)	f. went
7. buy	g. gave
8. build	h. met
9. give	i. bought

Look at the paragraphs about Gina's grandparents again and answer these questions.

1. Where did Gina's grandmother grow up?
2. Where did she go to school?
3. How did she get to school?
4. What did she do after school?
5. When did she meet her husband?
6. Where did they meet?
7. When did they get married?
8. What did they buy after they got married?
9. How many children did they have?
10. What kind of life did they have?

Interview a classmate. Find out about your classmate's parents or grandparents or another relative. 🔲

A: **Where did** *your grandfather* **grow up?**
B: *He* **grew up** *in a small town near Beijing.*

1. Where/grow up
   A: _____?
   B: _____.

2. How many brothers and sisters/have
   A: _____?
   B: _____.

3. What/have to do after school
   A: _____?
   B: _____.

4. Where/meet his wife (her husband)
   A: _____?
   B: _____.

5. When/get married
   A: _____?
   B: _____.

6. Ask your own question.
   A: _____?
   B: _____.

Listen and complete this conversation. 🔲

Lucy: You didn't come to class yesterday, Pravit. What happened?

Pravit: I ^{1}_____ a bad day yesterday so I stayed home. To begin with, I ^{2}_____ hear my alarm so I woke up ^{3}_____.

Lucy: Oh.

Pravit: I got up and got dressed ^{4}_____, but I put on one blue ^{5}_____ and one white sock so I had ^{6}_____ change my socks.

Lucy: Gee.

Pravit: That's not all. I fell in the ^{7}_____ and hit my head so I had to go to the ^{8}__ __. And I didn't have time to eat my breakfast.

Lucy: That's too bad.

Pravit: Yeah. And I forgot my ^{9}_____ so I had to go back ^{10}_____ again. ^{11}_____ on my way home, a police officer ^{12}_____ me a ticket.

Lucy: Wow! What did you do?

Pravit: ^{13}_____ I got home, I took off my ^{14}_____ , put on my pajamas, and went back to ^{15}_____!

What did Pravit do yesterday? Refer to exercise 4 and ask and answer questions.

A: **Did Pravit** *go to school* **yesterday?**
B: **No, he didn't. He** *stayed home.*

1. A: Pravit/wake up early yesterday

   B: _____.

2. A: he/put on two blue socks

   B: _____.

3. A: he/fall in the bathroom and hit his foot

   B: _____.

4. A: he/forget his books

   B: _____.

5. A: the police officer/give Pravit a newspaper

   B: _____.

Match the part of the sentence on the left with the part on the right.

1. I had a bad day
2. I got up late
3. I fell and hit my head
4. I had to change my socks
5. I forgot my wallet
6. I didn't have any food in the house
7. I didn't go to a restaurant for breakfast

a. so I had to go to the doctor.
b. because I put on one blue sock and one white sock.
c. so I didn't go to school.
d. because I didn't have any money.
e. so I didn't have any breakfast.
f. because I didn't hear my alarm.
g. so I had to go back home again.

Write a page in your diary. Tell what you did yesterday. Use the verbs in the list and your own verbs.

eat	take off
get dressed	go (back)
get up	wake up
put on	get (back)
do	have

Now report to the class what you did yesterday.

Famous dates and people

EXERCISE 1

Complete this conversation.

Mary: Hi, Bob. How [1]_____?
 Bob: Fine, thanks.
Mary: It's a beautiful day, [2]_____?
 Bob: Yes, [3]_____.
Mary: You aren't busy, [4]_____?
 Bob: No, [5]_____. I'm just reading my
         English notes.
Mary: [6]_____ have a test tomorrow?
 Bob: No, [7]_____, but this lesson
         is very interesting.

Now practice the conversation with a partner.
Use your partner's name in the first sentence.

EXERCISE 2

Listen to all of Mary's and Bob's conversation from exercise 1.
Choose the correct dates in the chart.

1. Columbus discovered America in _____.
   a. 1942   b. 1492   c. 1442

2. The United States declared its independence
   in _____.
   a. 1676   b. 1766   c. 1776

3. Alexander Graham Bell made the first
   telephone call in _____.
   a. 1876   b. 1886   c. 1776

4. Thomas Edison invented the light bulb
   in _____.
   a. 1879   b. 1779   c. 1869

5. Neil Armstrong and Edwin Aldrin walked on
   the moon in _____.
   a. 1869   b. 1969   c. 1960

Complete these sentences with *discover, travel, invent,* or *climb.* Be sure to use the correct tense.

1. In 1953, Sir Edmund Hillary _____ Mt. Everest.
2. Valentina Tereshkova _____ in space in 1963.
3. Sir Francis Drake _____ around the world from 1577 to 1580.
4. In 105, Ts'ai Lun _____ paper.
5. Roald Amundsen _____ to the South Pole in 1911.
6. Marie and Pierre Curie _____ radium in 1903.

Work with a group. Ask questions about famous people and events. Use *invent, make, discover,* and *build.* Look at the examples.

Who invented the telephone?
What did Thomas Edison invent?
When did Ts'ai Lun invent paper?

You are a newspaper reporter. Your partner is one of these famous people:

1. an astronaut who returned from . . .
2. a scientist who invented . . .
3. a doctor who discovered . . .
4. an explorer who discovered . . .
5. your own idea

Work together and write the questions you want to ask this person. Also write the person's answers. You can begin your questions with the words below.

Did/Do . . .   Where did . . .   Why did . . .   How long did . . .
Is/Are/Was/Were . . . When did . . .   What did . . .   Who . . .

When you finish, present your interview to the class.

An Interview with _____

A: _____?   A: _____?   A: _____?
B: _____.   B: _____.   B: _____.

GRAMMAR SUMMARY

TAG QUESTIONS: PRESENT TENSE

The cafeteria's a mess,	**isn't it?**	Yes, it is.
The students aren't cleaning now,	**are they?**	No, they aren't.
They don't like to clean,	**do they?**	No, they don't.
Mrs. Brennan likes parties,	**doesn't she?**	Yes, she does.

THE SIMPLE PAST TENSE
Negative Statements

Lucy and Gina Oscar	**didn't**	**clean** **close**	the tables. the windows.

Information (Wh-) Questions

How			**get** to school?
How many children	**did**	she	**have?**
What kind of life			**have?**

PAST TENSE OF IRREGULAR VERBS

Present Tense	Past Tense	Present Tense	Past Tense
build	**built**	grow up	**grew up**
buy	**bought**	have	**had**
come (back)	**came**	hear	**heard**
do	**did**	hit	**hit**
eat	**ate**	make	**made**
fall	**fell**	meet	**met**
forget	**forgot**	put on	**put on**
get (married/dressed)	**got**	take (care of)	**took**
give	**gave**	take off	**took off**
go (back)	**went**	wake up	**woke up**

WHO AS SUBJECT

Who invented the telephone?

ANYONE, SOMEONE, NO ONE

Did **anyone** fix the car?
Someone fixed the car.
No one fixed the refrigerator.

CONJUNCTIONS: SO AND BECAUSE

I had a bad day **so** I didn't go to school.
I got up late **because** I didn't hear my alarm.

VOCABULARY

alarm
astronaut
dance
decoration
electricity
explorer
extra
far
foreign
garbage
grandma
grandpa
head
independence
janitor
later
light bulb
midnight
moon
no one
pajamas
pretty
radium
scientist
so
someone
test
the South Pole
ticket
world
zoo

Gee.
Let's get started.
on my way home
That's too bad.
to begin with
Wow!

REGULAR VERBS

climb
declare
discover
end
guess
happen
invent
pick up (=clean)
remove
shop
turn off

IRREGULAR VERBS

build
buy
come (back)
do
eat
fall
forget
get (married/dressed)
give
go (back)
grow up
have
hear
hit
make
meet
put on
take care of
take off
wake up

For a complete list of irregular verbs, see page 123.

GUESSING WHAT HAPPENED

What happened?
 I guess Oscar didn't close the windows.

FINDING OUT WHO DID SOMETHING

Did anyone visit a foreign country last year?
 No one visited a foreign country last year.

TALKING ABOUT FAMILY AND FRIENDS

Where did your grandfather grow up?
 He grew up in a small town near Beijing.
Did Pravit go to school today?
 No, he didn't. He stayed home.

TALKING ABOUT FAMOUS PEOPLE AND EVENTS

Who invented the telephone?
 Alexander Graham Bell invented the telephone.
When did Ts'ai Lun invent paper?
 He invented paper in 105.
When did a man first walk on the moon?
 In 1969.

GIVING REASONS

I had a bad day so I didn't go to school.
I got up late because I didn't hear my alarm.

ASKING FOR CONFIRMATION

It's a beautiful day, isn't it?
 Yes, it is.
English isn't easy, is it?
 No, it isn't.
We don't speak English very well, do we?
 No, we don't.

Lynn's photo album

Look at the pictures. Then listen as you read the description of each picture.

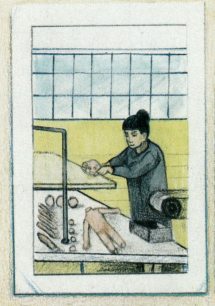

This is my mother. She worked in a doll factory before she married my father.

This is my sister. She went to medical school and became a doctor.

This is me five years ago. My parents gave me my first camera for my birthday.

This is my uncle. He wrote children's books. Parents around the world bought his books for their children. Now he's retired.

This is my cousin. He lived in the city for many years, but he didn't like the noise so now he lives in the country. He built a big house in the mountains.

Look at page 26 again and answer the questions.

> Who built a big house in the mountains?
>
> Lynn's cousin **did.**

1. Who wrote children's books?

2. Who worked in a doll factory?

3. Who went to medical school and became a doctor?

4. Who gave Lynn her first camera?

Now listen to the questions and answers.

Ask and answer questions with *Who.*

> walk to school today
>
> **A: Who** *walked to school today*?
> **B:** *I* **did.**

1. grow up in a big city
   A: _____
   B: _____

2. read an English newspaper this morning
   A: _____
   B: _____

3. have a party recently
   A: _____
   B: _____

4. write a letter last week
   A: _____
   B: _____

5. eat in a restaurant yesterday
   A: _____
   B: _____

6. Ask your own question.
   A: _____
   B: _____

EXERCISE 3

Read the conversation. Then choose the correct answer.

Keiko: Lynn, help ¹me with my homework, please.
Lynn: But I helped ²you last night.
Keiko: I know, but the homework is very difficult.
Lynn: Did you ask Mrs. Brennan for help?
Keiko: Yes. I talked to ³her after class, but I still don't understand ⁴it. By the way, did you develop the pictures of the class party?
Lynn: Yes, I did. Let's see. Where are they?
Keiko: Did you leave ⁵them at school?
Lynn: No, I don't think so. I met Oscar and Tony after school and I showed ⁶them the pictures. Then ... oh, Pierre has the pictures. I gave the pictures to ⁷him because he wanted to show the people at his restaurant.
Keiko: Oh. Well, I hope they give the pictures back to ⁸us soon. I really want to see them.

1. *me* refers to
   a. Lynn
   b. Keiko

2. *you* refers to
   a. Lynn
   b. Keiko

3. *her* refers to
   a. Mrs. Brennan
   b. Lynn

4. *it* refers to
   a. the class
   b. the homework

5. *them* refers to
   a. Oscar and Tony
   b. the pictures

6. *them* refers to
   a. Oscar and Tony
   b. the pictures

7. *him* refers to
   a. Oscar and Tony
   b. Pierre

8. *us* refers to
   a. Keiko
   b. Keiko and Lynn

Now listen to the conversation.

Look at Lynn's datebook and answer the questions. In your answers, use *him*, *her*, *it*, or *them* for the underlined words. Follow the example. 📼

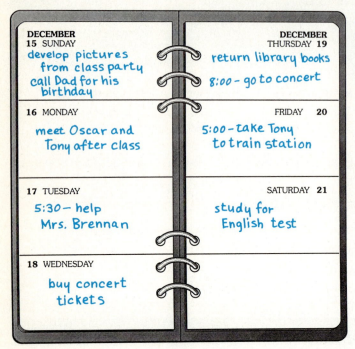

DECEMBER
15 SUNDAY
develop pictures
   from class party
call Dad for his
   birthday

16 MONDAY
meet Oscar and
   Tony after class

17 TUESDAY
5:30 – help
Mrs. Brennan

18 WEDNESDAY
buy concert
   tickets

DECEMBER
THURSDAY 19
return library books
8:00 – go to concert

FRIDAY 20
5:00 – take Tony
   to train station

SATURDAY 21
study for
English test

A: Did Lynn *develop the pictures from the class party?*
B: Yes. She *developed them on Sunday.*

1. Did Lynn call <u>her father</u> for his birthday?
2. Did Lynn meet <u>Oscar and Tony</u> after class?
3. Did Lynn help <u>Mrs. Brennan</u>?
4. Did Lynn buy <u>the tickets</u> for the concert?
5. Did Lynn return <u>the books</u> to the library?
6. Did Lynn go to <u>the concert</u>?
7. Did Lynn take <u>Tony</u> to the train station?
8. Did Lynn study for the <u>English test</u>?

Listen to the conversation and fill in the missing words. 📼

Keiko: Show ¹_____ the pictures of the party.
Lynn: Pierre has the pictures.
Keiko: No, he doesn't. I saw ²_____ last night.
Lynn: Oh, then you met ³_____.
Keiko: Who?
Lynn: Pierre's girlfriend.
Keiko: No. She wasn't with ⁴_____. What about the pictures?
Lynn: Well, then I don't remember what I did with ⁵_____.
Keiko: With what?
Lynn: My camera bag. I had my camera bag when I saw ⁶_____.
Keiko: Saw who?
Lynn: Oscar and Tony. I showed ⁷_____ the pictures. Then I put
        ⁸_____ in my camera bag. By the way, Oscar and Tony
        invited ⁹_____ to a picnic.
Keiko: Invited who? The class?
Lynn: No. ¹⁰_____ and ¹¹_____. Oscar thinks you're cute.
Keiko: What? Oscar and Tony both have girlfriends!
Lynn: I know, so I told ¹²_____ no.

Study the chart. Then complete Olga's letter to her sister Elsa. Use the correct word in the parentheses.

SUBJECT PRONOUN		OBJECT PRONOUN		POSSESSIVE ADJECTIVE	
I		me		my	
You		you		your	
He		him		his	
She	saw	her	and	her	mother.
It		it		its	
We		us		our	
They		them		their	

I saw **you** and **your** mother.

Dear Elsa,

How are (1 you/your)? (2 We/Us/Our) are all fine, but (3 we/us/our) are very busy in (4 we/us/our) new house.

Last weekend Hector and (5 I/me/my) painted the house and the garage. (6 He/Him/His) also tried to fix (7 he/him/his) car. Eddie helped (8 he/him/his). Unfortunately (9 it/its) still doesn't work and (10 they/them/their) don't know what's wrong with (11 it/its).

The kids are always busy. Saturday afternoon, (12 they/them/their) both went to a birthday party at (13 they/them/their) friend's house. Then (14 they/them/their) went to a movie with (15 we/us/our) on Saturday night. On Sunday Isabel did (16 she/her) homework and I helped (17 she/her). Eddie studied with (18 he/him/his) friend John. (19 I/Me/My) think (20 they/them/their) are happy here in Dallas, but (21 we/us/our) all miss (22 we/us/our) friends and family in Chile.

(23 I/Me/My) hope you can visit (24 we/us/our) next summer. Write to (25 I/me/my) soon!

Love,
Olga

Which one?

Look at the picture. Then listen as you read the conversation.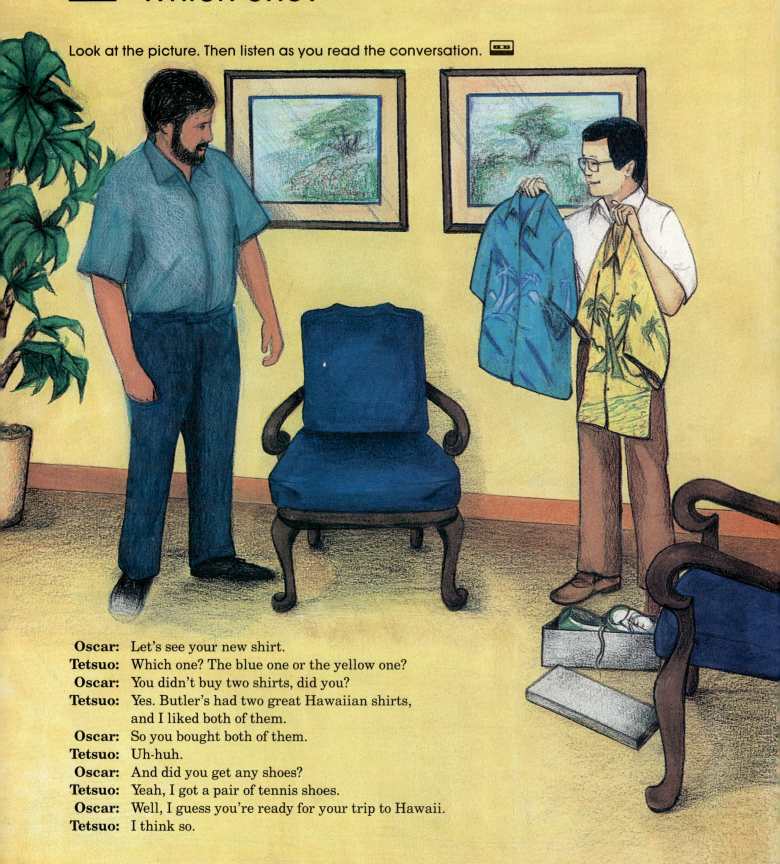

Oscar:	Let's see your new shirt.
Tetsuo:	Which one? The blue one or the yellow one?
Oscar:	You didn't buy two shirts, did you?
Tetsuo:	Yes. Butler's had two great Hawaiian shirts, and I liked both of them.
Oscar:	So you bought both of them.
Tetsuo:	Uh-huh.
Oscar:	And did you get any shoes?
Tetsuo:	Yeah, I got a pair of tennis shoes.
Oscar:	Well, I guess you're ready for your trip to Hawaii.
Tetsuo:	I think so.

Read the conversation on page 30 again. Are these statements True (T) or False (F)?

	T	F

1. Tetsuo didn't like the Hawaiian shirts at Butler's.
2. Tetsuo bought two shirts.
3. Butler's is a store.
4. Tetsuo didn't get any shoes.
5. Tetsuo is going to Hawaii.
6. Oscar is going to Hawaii.

Pretend you want to buy these items. Tell the salesperson which ones you want. Listen to the examples.

little gray   little white

red/with high heels   white

buy a kitten

Salesperson:	May I help you?
Customer:	Yes. I'd like to *buy a kitten*.
Salesperson:	Which one?
Customer:	The *little gray one*.

try on some shoes

Salesperson:	May I help you?
Customer:	Yes. I'd like to *try on some shoes*.
Salesperson:	Which ones?
Customer:	The *red ones with high heels*.

gray/ with two doors

black/ with four doors

1. buy that car

traditional   modern

2. buy some dining room chairs

with nuts   chocolate

3. buy some cookies

dark gray

light gray

4. try on those gloves

blue plaid/ with short sleeves   green striped/ with long sleeves

5. buy a shirt

brown   brown and white

6. buy a puppy

Listen and choose the correct answer. 📼

1. Which dog did the people take?
   a. the small one
   b. the big one

2. Which earrings did Lucy buy?
   a. the silver ones
   b. the gold ones

3. Which shirts did Tetsuo buy?
   a. the ones with short sleeves
   b. the ones with long sleeves

4. Which car did Hector and Olga buy?
   a. the one with four doors
   b. the one with two doors

5. Which movie did the students see?
   a. the one in Spanish
   b. the one in English

6. Which sunglasses did Roberto buy?
   a. the gray ones
   b. the green ones

EXERCISE 4

Ask questions and find out if your partner agrees with your answers in exercise 3. 📼

A: The people **took** the small dog, **didn't they?** **B:** Yes, they did.	OR	**A:** The people **didn't take** the big dog, **did they?** **B:** No, they didn't.

1. A: Lucy got the silver earrings, _____?

   B: _____.

2. A: Tetsuo didn't buy the shirts with long sleeves, _____?

   B: _____.

3. A: Hector and Olga bought the car with four doors, _____?

   B: _____.

4. A: The students saw a movie in English, _____?

   B: _____

5. A: Roberto didn't buy the gray ones, _____?

   B: _____.

Now listen to each exchange. 📼

EXERCISE 5

Talk to your classmates. Find someone who . . .

1. bought some new shoes recently.
2. went to a concert recently.
3. doesn't like cats.
4. would like to buy a new car.
5. has a car with four doors.
6. is taking a trip soon.
7. would like to go to Hawaii.
8. didn't do the homework last night.

May I help you?

Ask and answer questions about the store directory.

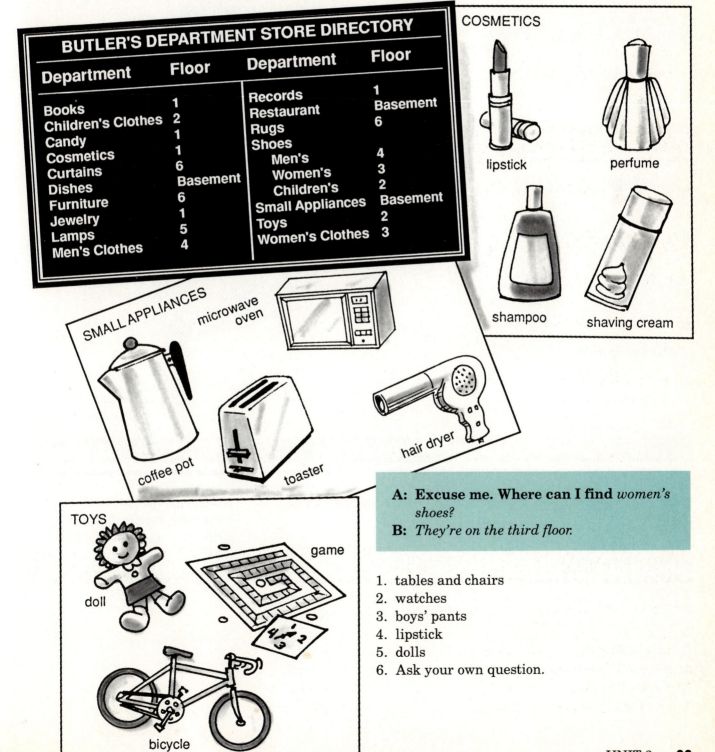

BUTLER'S DEPARTMENT STORE DIRECTORY

Department	Floor	Department	Floor
Books	1	Records	1
Children's Clothes	2	Restaurant	Basement
Candy	1	Rugs	6
Cosmetics	1	Shoes	
Curtains	6	Men's	4
Dishes	Basement	Women's	3
Furniture	6	Children's	2
Jewelry	1	Small Appliances	Basement
Lamps	5	Toys	2
Men's Clothes	4	Women's Clothes	3

COSMETICS

lipstick

perfume

shampoo

shaving cream

SMALL APPLIANCES

microwave oven

coffee pot

toaster

hair dryer

TOYS

doll

game

bicycle

A: **Excuse me. Where can I find** *women's shoes?*
B: *They're on the third floor.*

1. tables and chairs
2. watches
3. boys' pants
4. lipstick
5. dolls
6. Ask your own question.

First try to complete the conversation with the sentences in the list. Then listen and check your answers.

a. Can I try it on?
b. Yes. I'm looking for a sweater.
c. Cash or charge?
d. Yes. Here you are.
e. A medium, I think.
f. How does it fit?
g. Green. Dark green.

Saleswoman:	May I help you?
Man:	1_____
Saleswoman:	What size?
Man:	2_____
Saleswoman:	What color are you looking for?
Man:	3_____
Saleswoman:	Here's a nice one.
Man:	4_____
Saleswoman:	Certainly. The dressing room is right over there.

Saleswoman:	5_____
Man:	It's too tight. Do you have a large?
Saleswoman:	6_____
Man:	It's fine. I'll take it.
Saleswoman:	7_____
Man:	Charge.

Match the questions on the left with the best responses on the right.

1. May I help you?
2. What size?
3. What color are you looking for?
4. Can I try it on?
5. How does it fit?
6. It's too tight. Do you have a medium?
7. Cash or charge?

a. Blue, I think.
b. Charge.
c. Yes. I'm looking for a shirt.
d. Certainly. The dressing room is right over there.
e. Fine. I'll take it.
f. Yes. Here you are.
g. A small.

Now pretend you are shopping for clothes and practice the conversation in exercise 2. If you don't want any help, you can say *I'm just looking, thank you.*

Look at the application for a charge account at Butler's Department Store and answer the questions.

BUTLER'S

TYPE OF ACCOUNT—PLEASE CHECK ONE	FOR OFFICE USE ONLY
☐ INDIVIDUAL ACCOUNT	
☐ JOINT ACCOUNT	APPLICATION

1. YOU

NAME	LAST	FIRST	MIDDLE INITIAL	AGE	SOC. SEC. NO.
NO. AND STREET		APT	HOW LONG?		TELEPHONE
CITY AND STATE		ZIP CODE	☐ OWN ☐ RENT ☐ WITH PARENTS ☐ OTHER		

PRESENT BUSINESS OR EMPLOYER	TYPE OF BUSINESS	HOW LONG?	POSITION
BUSINESS ADDRESS	CITY	STATE	ZIP CODE	BUSINESS TELEPHONE	SALARY

2. JOINT APPLICATION

LAST NAME	FIRST	MIDDLE INITIAL	AGE	RELATION TO
PRESENT BUSINESS OR EMPLOYER	TYPE OF BUSINESS	HOW LONG?	
BUSINESS ADDRESS	CITY	STATE	ZIP

3. YOUR CREDIT

		BANK	ADDRESS	CREDIT CARDS
IF NONE	CHECKING ACCT.			

BUTLER'S
0652 6673150
Signature

1. An *individual account* is an account for
   a. only you.
   b. you and someone in your family.

2. A *joint account* is an account for
   a. only you.
   b. you and someone in your family.

3. *For office use only* means
   a. write here.
   b. don't write here.

4. *Present business* means
   a. where you work now.
   b. where you worked before.

5. *Employer* means
   a. you.
   b. the company you work for.

6. *Salary* means
   a. the money you get for your work.
   b. the number of days you work each week.

Now complete the application for a charge account.

VOCABULARY

WHO AS SUBJECT AND SHORT ANSWERS

Who	wrote children's books?	Lynn's uncle **did**.
	walked to school today?	I **did**.

ONE AND ONES

The red **one**.
The **ones** with high heels.

INFORMATION (WH-) QUESTIONS WITH WHICH

Which	dog did they take? one?	The small one.
	shirts did Tetsuo buy? ones?	The ones with short sleeves.

OBJECT PRONOUNS

Did they see	me? you? him? her? it? us? them?

WOULD LIKE TO

I	**'d like to**	**buy**	a kitten.

TAG QUESTIONS: SIMPLE PAST TENSE

Lucy	got the silver earrings,	**didn't she?**	Yes, she did.
She	didn't get the gold ones,	**did she?**	No, she didn't.

appliance
application
bicycle
cosmetics
cute
dark (color)
develop
dressing room
employer
gold
high heels
individual/joint account
jewelry
kitten
light (color)
lipstick
little
medical school
medium
modern
mountain
none
noise
perfume
picnic
present
puppy
recently
retired
salary
shampoo
shaving cream
sleeve
traditional
toaster
toy
trip
type
use

both of them
By the way,
Unfortunately,

VOCABULARY

VERBS*
become [became]
hope
leave [left]
look for
mean [meant]
read [read]
refer
try on
write [wrote]

COMPOUND NOUNS

Many times in this unit you saw two nouns together, with one noun describing the other noun. These are called compound nouns.

camera bag
charge account
class party
coffee pot
concert tickets
credit card
department store
doll factory
English test
hair dryer
homework
library books
microwave oven
photo album
silver earrings
tennis shoes
train station

*The past tense of irregular verbs is in brackets. For a complete list of irregular verbs, see page 123.

COMMUNICATION SUMMARY

TALKING ABOUT THE PAST

Who grew up in a big city?
   I did.
Did Lynn develop the pictures of the class party?
   Yes. She developed them on Sunday.

ASKING FOR AND GIVING ASSISTANCE

Excuse me. Where can I find toys?
   They're on the second floor.

May I help you?
   I'm looking for a sweater.
   I'd like to try on some shoes.
   I'd like to buy a kitten.
   I'm just looking, thank you.
What color are you looking for?
   Dark green.

I'll take it.
   Cash or charge?
Charge.

IDENTIFYING

Which shirts did Tetsuo buy?
   The ones with short sleeves.
Which one?
   The little gray one.
Which ones?
   The red ones with high heels.

ASKING FOR CONFIRMATION

Lucy got the silver earrings, didn't she?
   Yes, she did.
She didn't get the gold ones, did she?
   No, she didn't.

TALKING ABOUT SIZE AND FIT

What size?
   A medium.
Can I try it on?
   Certainly. The dressing room is right over there.

How does it fit?
   It's fine.
   It's too tight. Do you have a large?

There was a robbery last night.

Spike often has trouble with the police. Look at the picture. Then listen as you read the conversation.

Detective: Spike, there was a robbery at United Bank last night.

Spike: So?

Detective: So where were you at 10 o'clock?

Spike: I was home.

Detective: Who were you with?

Spike: Nobody. I was alone.

Detective: Were you and your wife together last night?

Spike: No. Belle wasn't there. She was out.

Detective: Out? At 10 o'clock at night?

Spike: Yeah. She and a friend were at Butler's. There was a big sale—a lot of things were very cheap. Anyway, the store was open until midnight. And that's when she got home.

Was or were? Read the conversation on page 38 again. Then choose the correct word in parentheses.

1. There (was/were) a robbery at United Bank last night.
2. The detective asked, "So where (was/were) you at 10 o'clock?"
3. Spike (was/were) at home at 10 o'clock.
4. Belle and her friend (was/were) at Butler's.
5. There (was/were) a big sale.
6. A lot of things (was/were) very cheap.
7. The store (was/were) open until midnight.
8. Spike (was/were) alone.

Spike's wife, Belle, is talking to the police. Complete her conversation with *was*, *wasn't* (*was not*), *were*, and *weren't* (*were not*).

I **wasn't** home last night.
My husband **wasn't** with me.
My friend Dolores **was** with me.
It **was** late.
There **was** a big sale.

We **were** at Butler's Department Store.
Were you at Butler's, too?
There **were** dresses on sale.
They **were** beautiful.
They **weren't** expensive.

"I ¹_____ home last night. My friend Dolores and I ²_____ at Butler's because there ³_____ a big sale. I went shopping for my family, but I bought some things for myself, too. It ⁴_____ wonderful! The shoes ⁵_____ on sale! The sweaters ⁶_____ on sale! The dresses ⁷_____ beautiful! The coats ⁸_____ cheap! There ⁹_____ pocketbooks in every color! There ¹⁰_____ something for everyone! I even bought a piano!

Spike hates department stores so he ¹¹_____ with me. He ¹²_____ home in the living room in front of the television. He was there all night. I remember very well because it ¹³_____ late when I got home and Spike ¹⁴_____ very angry."

Now listen to Belle's side of the conversation.

Listen to the questions about Spike and Belle. Choose the correct answers.

1. a. Yes, they were.
   b. No, they weren't.

2. a. Yes, he was.
   b. No, he wasn't.

3. a. Yes, he was.
   b. No, he wasn't.

4. a. Yes, she was.
   b. No, she wasn't.

5. a. Yes, they were.
   b. No, they weren't.

6. a. Yes, they were.
   b. No, they weren't.

7. a. Yes, there was.
   b. No, there wasn't.

8. a. Yes, they were.
   b. No, they weren't.

9. a. Yes, it was.
   b. No, it wasn't.

10. a. Yes, he was.
    b. No, he wasn't.

Complete the conversations. Then listen to them.

Belle/at home last night?

A: Was Belle at home last night?
B: No, she wasn't.
A: Where was she?
B: She was at Butler's.

1. Gina/in class last night?
   A: _____?
   B: _____.
   A: _____?
   B: _____.

2. Lucy/at work last week?
   A: _____?
   B: _____.
   A: _____?
   B: _____.

3. Ann and Jerry/at the movies on Sunday?
   A: _____?
   B: _____.
   A: _____?
   B: _____.

4. Oscar/at the hospital this morning?
   A: _____?
   B: _____.
   A: _____?
   B: _____.

5. Joe and Moe/at the library last night?
   A: _____?
   B: _____.
   A: _____?
   B: _____.

Marco thinks he saw the bank robbers, so he is talking to the police. Work in a group and read Marco's description of the three robbers. Then match the description with the correct picture.

Officer: So, Mr. Martinez, what did they look like?

Marco: [1]Well, one was average height and had blue eyes. He was very young, but he was bald and he had a mustache. He had on a dark brown jacket, green pants, and a funny red cap. He also had an earring in his right ear.

Officer: What about his friends?

Marco: [2]One was tall and thin. He had very short blond hair and a beard. He had on plaid pants and a striped shirt. And he wore four rings on his left hand.

Officer: What about the other one?

Marco: [3]I remember this one very well. He was very short and fat. He was old and wore glasses. He had one red shoe and one blue one. And he had on red shorts and a sweater.

Officer: And the fourth robber? What did he look like?

Marco: She.

Officer: Do you mean there was a woman?

Marco: Yes.

Now write your own description of the fourth robber.

EXERCISE 6

Two police officers are talking. Complete their conversation. Then listen to it. 🔲

Officer 1: So, Mr. Martinez **was** at the bank last night, **wasn't he**?

Officer 2: Yes, he was.

Officer 1: And according to Mr. Martinez, there **were** three robbers, **weren't there**?

Officer 2: No. There were four robbers.

Officer 1: So, there were four men, [1]_____?

Officer 2: No. There were three men.

Officer 1: Oh. Well, there was one woman, [2]_____?

Officer 2: Yes, there was.

Officer 1: One man was bald, [3]_____?

Officer 2: Yes, he was.

Officer 1: The other men weren't bald, [4]_____?

Officer 2: No, they weren't.

Officer 1: And one man had on an earring, [5]_____?

Officer 2: Yes, he did.

Continue and ask your own questions about the robbers.

LESSON 2

Let's buy a small car!

Look at the picture. Then listen as you read the conversation.

Jerry:	I think you need a new car.
Ann:	Let's buy a small car!
Jerry:	But small cars aren't as comfortable as big cars.
Ann:	All right. Let's buy a big car!
Jerry:	However, small cars are easier to drive than big cars.
Ann:	Then let's buy a small car!
Jerry:	But big cars are safer than small cars.
Ann:	OK, a big car.
Jerry:	But I don't know. Small cars are more economical than big cars.
Ann:	OK, a small one.
Jerry:	But big cars are faster than small cars.
Ann:	Well, which one is better, a small car or a big car?
Jerry:	I can't make up my mind.
Ann:	You know, Jerry, I have an idea. Let's not buy a car at all! I'll take the bus!

Read the conversation on page 42 again. Then answer *That's right*, *That's wrong*, or *It doesn't say*.

1. Ann and Jerry want to buy a car.
2. Jerry thinks big cars are comfortable.
3. He thinks small cars are difficult to drive.
4. He likes four-door cars.
5. Ann thinks small cars are safe.
6. Jerry can't decide about the car.

Complete the sentences. Then listen and check your answers.

> **big**
>
> The blue car **is as big as** the red one.
> The blue car **isn't as big as** the green one.
> The red car **isn't as big as** the green one, either.

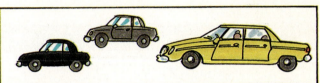

1. comfortable

   The black car _____ the gray one.
   The black car _____ the yellow one.
   The gray car _____ the yellow one, either.

2. tall

   The building on the left _____ the one in the middle.
   The building on the left _____ the one on the right.
   The one in the middle _____ the one on the right, either.

3. fast

   The car on the left _____ the one in the middle.
   The car on the left _____ the one on the right.
   The car in the middle _____ the one on the right, either.

4. expensive

   The blue sweater _____ the red one.
   The blue sweater _____ the green one.
   The red sweater _____ the green one, either.

5. good

   The Arrow _____ the NRC.
   The Arrow _____ the Videomax.
   The NRC _____ the Videomax, either.

Agree or disagree with the statements.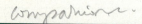

> **A: Cats aren't as friendly as dogs.**
> **B: I agree. I don't think** *cats are as*
> *friendly as dogs, either.*
> OR
> **I don't agree. I think** *cats are just as*
> *friendly as dogs.*

1. Teachers are as important as doctors.
2. Classical music isn't as good as rock music.
3. Love is as important as money.
4. Soccer is as exciting as baseball.
5. Women aren't as strong as men.
6. Ice cream isn't as healthy as fruit.

Look at the picture and the chart, and then make sentences.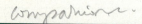

> The Astro/small
> The Astro is **smaller than** the Deville.
>
> The Deville/expensive
> The Deville is more **expensive than** the Astro.

The **ASTRO**
• small
• economical
• cheap
• easy to drive

The **DEVILLE**
• big
• comfortable
• fast
• good — but expensive

1. The Astro/cheap
2. The Astro/easy to drive
3. The Deville/comfortable
4. The Deville/fast
5. The Deville/good
6. The Deville/big
7. The Astro/economical

fast—fast**er**	economical—**more** economical
small—small**er**	expensive—**more** expensive
cheap—cheap**er**	comfortable—**more** comfortable
big—bigg**er**	
easy—easi**er**	good—**better**

Give your opinion. Answer the questions.

> **A:** A car is safe to drive. What about a motorcycle?
> **B:** A motorcycle isn't as safe to drive (as a car).
> OR
> A motorcycle is safer to drive (than a car).

1. A motorcycle is dangerous to drive. What about a car?
2. A big car is comfortable to drive. What about a small car?
3. Fruit is good to eat. What about vegetables?
4. An apartment is easy to clean. What about a house?
5. English is hard to learn. What about your language?
6. Actors and actresses are interesting to meet. What about musicians?

Listen and complete the conversation.

Man:	Let's take our vacation in the city this year.
Woman:	But the weather in the country is ¹_____ the weather in the city.
Man:	All right. Let's take our vacation in the country.
Woman:	But life in the city is ²_____ life in the country.
Man:	Then let's take our vacation in the city.
Woman:	But the country is ³_____ the city for children.
Man:	OK, the country.
Woman:	However, the people in the city are ⁴_____ the people in the country. And the restaurants are ⁵_____ the restaurants in the country.
Man:	All right then. The city.
Woman:	But the people in the country are ⁶_____ the people in the city.
Man:	Please make up your mind!
Woman:	I can't.
Man:	You know, I have an idea. Let's not take a vacation at all! Let's stay home!

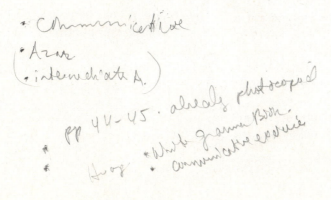

Sale!

EXERCISE 1

Pretend you are the security guard in the picture. Answer the police officer's questions.

1. How many robbers were there?
2. Were they all men?
3. How many customers were there in the store?
4. What time was the robbery?
5. How much money did the robbers take?
6. Did the robbers have guns?

EXERCISE 2

Read the article and guess the missing words. Then listen and correct your guesses. 🔲

GIVE ME AN APARTMENT ANY DAY!

A lot of people think that a **1**_____ is nicer than an apartment. I don't agree. I prefer an apartment. I lived in an **2**_____ for many years. The rooms were small, but they were very **3**_____ . And I didn't need much furniture. The building was **4**_____ the bus stop, so it was easy to get to **5**_____ . The building was very modern, and my rent wasn't **6**_____ . My neighbors were **7**_____ .

Two years **8**_____ , I moved to a **9**_____ . The house is nice, but I pay a lot of **10**_____ to the bank every month. The rooms are very big, and I had to buy a lot of **11**_____ . The house is **12**_____ far from transportation, so it isn't **13**_____ to get to work. And I'm lonely. I never see my **14**_____ .

EXERCISE 3

Discuss these questions.

1. According to the author of *Give Me an Apartment Any Day!*, which is better, a house or an apartment?
2. Why does the author prefer this?
3. Which do you prefer, a house or an apartment? Why?

Read the department store ads and answer the questions.

VALENTINE'S DAY SALE

MEN'S COTTON SWEATERS
All sizes ● $10 - $20 (were $30)

WOMEN'S SILK BLOUSES
All sizes, all colors
$15 (were $25)

**MEN'S AND WOMEN'S
LEATHER SHOES**
$25

LEW'S
112 East 10th Street
OPEN MONDAY from 9 to 9

VALENTINE'S DAY SALE

*BEAUTIFUL COTTON
SWEATERS FOR MEN*
*Sizes small, medium, large
NOW ONLY $40
(were $75)*

*ALL SILK BLOUSES
Red and black
ONLY $35
(were $75)*

*IMPORTED SHOES
FOR MEN AND WOMEN
$70*

The Grandway

285 Park Avenue
OPEN MONDAY from **10** to **6**

1. Which store sells cheaper clothes?
2. Which store do you think is bigger?
3. Which store do you think is in a more expensive neighborhood?

4. Which store would you like to receive a gift from? Why?
5. Is there a store like Lew's or The Grandway where you live? Describe that store.

Find out your classmate's opinions. Ask and answer questions.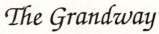

intelligent/a cat or a dog?
A: Which is more intelligent, a cat or a dog?
B: A cat is more intelligent than a dog.
(A cat is just as intelligent as a dog.)

1. easy/English or your language?
2. important/money or good health?
3. bad for you/smoking or drinking?
(Note: bad → worse)
4. dangerous/travel by car or travel by plane?

THE PAST TENSE: *BE*

Information (Wh-) Questions

Where	**were**	you?
	was	he/she/it?
	were	we/you/they?

Statements

I	**was**	at home.
He/She/It	**wasn't (was not)**	
You/We/They	**were** **weren't (were not)**	

Yes/No Questions

Were	you	
Was	he she it	at home?
Were	we you they	

Short Answers

Yes,	I he she it	**was.**	No,	I he she it	**wasn't.**
	you we they	**were.**		you we they	**weren't.**

Tag Questions

There was a robbery,	**wasn't there?**	Yes, there was.
Spike wasn't at the bank,	**was he?**	No, he wasn't.
There were four robbers,	**weren't there?**	Yes, there were.
The robbers weren't women,	**were they?**	No, they weren't.

There was/There were

There	**was (wasn't)**	a robbery last night.
	were (weren't)	four robbers.

(NOT) AS . . . AS

The blue car is **as big as** the red one.
Cats aren't **as friendly as** dogs.

ADJECTIVE + *TO* **+ VERB**

An apartment is **easy to clean**.
A motorcycle isn't as **safe to drive** (as a car).
A car is **safer to drive** (than a motorcycle).

THE COMPARATIVE OF ADJECTIVES

A small car is	cheap**er** nic**er** eas**ier** to drive **more** economical **better**	**than**	a big car.
	worse		

VOCABULARY

bus stop
cap
coat
cotton
drinking
ear
gun
hand
health
however
idea
imported
language
leather
line
motorcycle
myself
neighbor
nobody
rent
robber
robbery
sale
shorts
silk
smoking
soccer
travel

according to
All right.
Anyway,
by car/plane
I can't make up my mind.
in the middle
Let's not . . .
not . . . at all
on sale
on the left/right
Valentine's Day

VOCABULARY

ADJECTIVES

better (good)
cheap
comfortable
difficult
economical
exciting
expensive
friendly
funny
healthy
important
safe
strong
worse (bad)

VERBS

be [was/were] far from
be out (= not be home)
choose [chose]
decide about
drive [drove]
go [went] shopping
hate
have [had] on
look like
move
pay [paid]
prefer
receive
take [took] a vacation

WAYS TO DESCRIBE PEOPLE

be average height/short/tall
be bald
be fat/thin
have a beard/mustache
have blue eyes
have short blond hair
wear a ring/glasses
have on red shorts
be old/young

COMMUNICATION SUMMARY

TALKING ABOUT THE PAST

There was a robbery last night.
Were Spike and Belle together last night?
    No, they weren't.
    Belle and Dolores were at Butler's.
    Spike was at home.

DESCRIBING PEOPLE

What did he look like?
    He was tall and thin. He had short blond hair and a beard. And he had
    blue eyes. He had on plaid pants and a striped shirt.

COMPARING

Big cars are safer than small cars.
Big cars are more expensive than small cars.
Small cars are easier to drive than big cars.
Cats aren't as friendly as dogs.

AGREEING AND DISAGREEING

Cats aren't as friendly as dogs.
    I agree. I don't think cats are as friendly as dogs, either.
    I don't agree. I think cats are just as friendly as dogs.

EMPHASIZING

Cats are just as friendly as dogs.
I even bought a piano!

MAKING SUGGESTIONS

Let's buy a small car.
Let's not buy a car at all.

TALKING ABOUT PREFERENCES

Which do you prefer, a house or an apartment?
    I prefer an apartment because it's easier to clean.

LESSON 1

He has the worst prices!

Look at the picture. Then listen as you read the conversation.

Buy a car from

Bargain Bill!

We sell the cheapest cars in Dallas!
Our prices are the best!
Our salesmen are the
friendliest!
Our finance rates are the
lowest!

Gina: Hi, Carlos. What's the matter?
Carlos: Well, I just came back from Bargain Bill's.
Gina: Bargain Bill's? Are you buying a new car?
Carlos: I'm thinking about it.
Gina: Why are you upset? He has the best prices in Dallas, doesn't he?
Carlos: No! He has the worst prices! His cars are the most expensive. His finance rates are the highest! His salesmen are the rudest, and I don't think they're honest.
Gina: That's terrible.

Read the conversation on page 50 again. Then give your opinion. Answer *I think so* or *I don't think so.*

1. Bargain Bill sells new cars.
2. Bill is a nice man.
3. Carlos liked Bargain Bill.
4. Bill has honest salesmen.
5. Bill's customers are usually unhappy.
6. Bargain Bill is very successful.

First look at the examples below. Then complete the conversation and the ad.

> Toy Town is **the newest** store in Dallas.
> It has **the nicest** toys.
> It is **the biggest** toy store around here.
> It is **the busiest** toy store around here.
> It is **the most successful** toy store in Texas.
> It is **the best** toy store around here.

Marco: Hi, Olga. What's the matter?
Olga: Well, I just came back from Toy Town.

Marco: Toy Town? They have (**1.** wonderful) toys in Dallas, right?
Olga: Wrong! They have (**2.** small) selection of toys! And their toys are (**3.** dangerous) ones around! Toy Town is really (**4.** bad) toy store in Dallas.
Marco: That's terrible. The ad says Toy Town is (**5.** big) toy store in Texas.
Olga: Well, the people of Toy Town aren't honest, because their ad isn't correct. It isn't big at all!

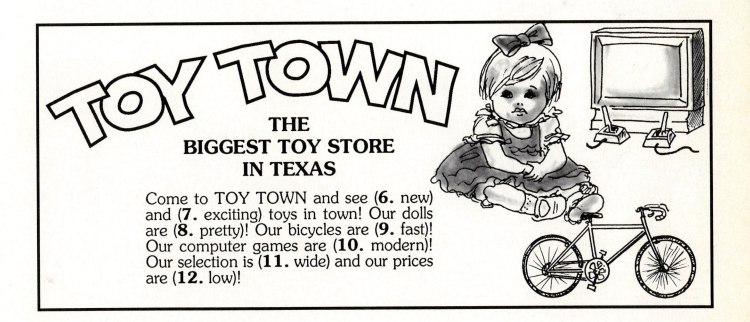

TOY TOWN

THE BIGGEST TOY STORE IN TEXAS

Come to TOY TOWN and see (**6.** new) and (**7.** exciting) toys in town! Our dolls are (**8.** pretty)! Our bicycles are (**9.** fast)! Our computer games are (**10.** modern)! Our selection is (**11.** wide) and our prices are (**12.** low)!

Now listen to the conversation.

What's the problem? First listen to the example. Then listen to the conversations and complete the sentences. 📼

> These shoes **aren't the most comfortable** in the world. In fact, they **aren't comfortable** at all.

1. This computer game _____ in the world. In fact, it _____ at all.
2. These books _____ in the world. In fact, they _____ at all.
3. This pillow _____ in the world. In fact, it _____ at all.
4. These curtains _____ in the world. In fact, they _____ at all.

Look at the pictures and practice the conversation. Listen to the example. 📼

> A: May I help you?
> B: Yes, please. I'd like to return *this computer game.*
> A: Sure. What's the problem with *it?*
> B: Your ad says *it's the easiest computer game* in the world, but *it isn't easy at all.*

① These books aren't interesting at all.

② These curtains aren't pretty at all.

③ This pillow isn't soft at all.

④ These apples aren't delicious at all.

Roberto wants to buy a computer so he can work at home. Read the lists he made. The lists compare three computer stores.

Now complete the sentences and compare the stores. Use the comparative (*smaller/more expensive than*), the superlative (*the smallest/most expensive*), or as . . . as (*as small/expensive as*). Look at the examples.

> The selection at The Input is **smaller than** the selection at Computer World.
> Computer World is **as close as** Fast Frank's.
> Computers at The Input are **the cheapest**.

1. The finance rate at The Input is (high) the finance rate at Computer World.
2. The selection at Computer World is (big) the selection at The Input.
3. The Input is (far) store from Roberto's house.
4. The selection at The Input is not (big) the selection at Computer World.
5. The finance rate at Fast Frank's is (low) of the three.
6. The salespeople at Fast Frank's are (friendly) the salespeople at Computer World.
7. The prices at The Input are (good) the prices at Fast Frank's.
8. In your opinion, which is the best place to buy a computer? Why?

Interview a classmate and take notes. Then report your findings to the class.

> A: **What do you think is** *the most exciting sport*?
> B: *Soccer*. (**I think** *soccer* **is** *the most exciting sport*.)

1. the most exciting sport
2. the fastest way to travel
3. the best movie
4. the dirtiest city
5. the most delicious food
6. Ask your own question.

Why don't you go home and rest?

Look at the picture. Then listen as you read the conversation.

Mrs. Brennan:	Hi, Oscar. I'm sorry I'm late. I don't feel very well today.
Oscar:	I'm sorry to hear that. What's the matter?
Mrs. Brennan:	I have a headache and a sore throat. I think I have a fever, too.
Oscar:	Why don't you go home and rest? And if you have a headache and a fever, take two aspirin.
Mrs. Brennan:	No, I can't do that. What about class? Say, where are all the students?
Oscar:	Well, they're sick, too. I think everybody has the flu—or a bad cold. They all have headaches, sore throats, and runny noses.
Mrs. Brennan:	Oh, that's too bad.
Oscar:	Everybody except Tetsuo.
Mrs. Brennan:	What's the matter with Tetsuo?
Oscar:	He had a car accident. He hurt his arm and broke his leg.
Mrs. Brennan:	Oh, no!

EXERCISE 1

Answer *That's right, That's wrong,* or *It doesn't say* and correct the wrong answers. Look at the example.

> Mrs. Brennan feels fine today.
> That's wrong. She doesn't feel very well today.

1. Mrs. Brennan has a headache.
2. Oscar wants Mrs. Brennan to go home.
3. Oscar wants Mrs. Brennan to take three aspirin.
4. All the students are sick except Oscar.
5. Oscar had a car accident.
6. Tetsuo hit a bus with his car.
7. Tetsuo broke his leg.

EXERCISE 2

Work with a group. Label the parts of the body. Use the words in the list.

PARTS OF THE BODY

head
forehead
eye
nose
ear
tooth (teeth)
mouth
cheek
chin
neck
shoulder
arm
elbow
wrist
finger
thumb
hand
chest
stomach
back
hip
leg
knee
ankle
foot (feet)
toe

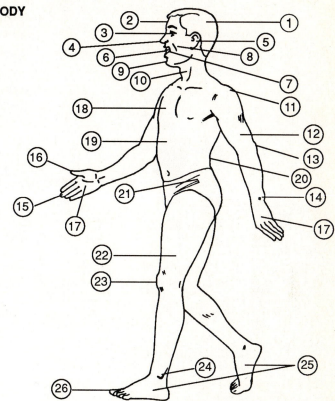

EXERCISE 3

What's the matter with Oscar's patients? Listen to the example. Then listen and complete the conversations. 🔲

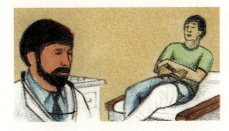

> Oscar: **What's the matter?**
> Tetsuo: *I hurt my arm.*
> Oscar: **Oh, that's too bad.**

1. Oscar: What's the matter, Mr. Brennan?
   Jerry: _____.
   Oscar: Oh, that's too bad.

2. Oscar: What's the matter?
   Olga: _____.
   Oscar: I'm sorry to hear that.

3. Oscar: What's the matter, Tony?
   Tony: _____.
   Oscar: Oh, that's too bad.

4. Oscar: What's the matter?
   Lynn: _____.
   Oscar: Oh, I'm sorry to hear that.

5. Oscar: What's the matter, Susan?
   Susan: _____.
   Oscar: Oh, that's too bad.

6. Oscar: What's the matter?
   Pravit: _____.
   Oscar: Well, I'm sorry to hear that.

What's the matter with these people? Give the best description for each person. You can use some of the words in the list.

has a stomachache	has a sore throat	broke her nose
a headache	a runny nose	cut her finger
a backache	a cold	hurt her back
a toothache	a cough	
	a fever	
	the flu	

①

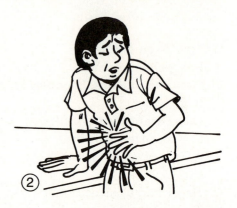
②

He *has a sore throat.*

③

④

⑤

⑥

⑦

⑧

Match each problem on the left with the best solution on the right.

1. If you have a headache,
2. If you have a sore throat,
3. If you have a cold,
4. If you have a toothache,
5. If you hurt your back,
6. If you fall and hit your head,

a. drink juice, take vitamins, and rest.
b. go to the dentist.
c. lie down and rest.
d. call the doctor immediately.
e. take two aspirin.
f. don't talk a lot.

Now say what you do. Look at the example.

> **A:** What do you do **if** you have a headache?
> **B:** **If** I have a headache, I take two aspirin.
> OR
> I take two aspirin **if** I have a headache.

1. What do you do if you have a sore throat?
2. What do you do if you have a cold?
3. What do you do if you have a toothache?
4. What do you do if you hurt your back?
5. Do you have solutions for other medical problems?

Make suggestions for your partner's problems. Listen to the examples.

> **A:** **I don't understand this exercise.**
> **B:** **Why don't you** *talk to the teacher about it*?
> **A:** **That's a good idea. (That's a good suggestion.)**

A: I have a headache.
B: Why don't you _____?
A: _____.

A: I don't like my job.
B: Why don't you _____?
A: _____.

A: I don't feel well.
B: Why don't you _____?
A: _____.

A: I bought a computer at Computer World, and I don't like it.
B: Why don't you _____?
A: _____.

A: I hurt my head.
B: Why don't you _____?
A: _____.

Tell your own problem.
A: _____.
B: _____?
A: _____.

What seems to be the problem?

Read the directions on the different bottles. Then answer the questions.

ⓐ

DIRECTIONS:
Take one teaspoon
after every meal.
Do not take more
than four teaspoons
a day.
NOT for children.

ⓑ

DOSAGE: Adults, 1
to 2 tablets 3 or 4
times daily for colds,
fevers, headaches,
and other aches and
pains. Children
(6-12), ½ to 1 tablet 3
or 4 times daily.

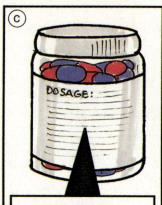

ⓒ

DOSAGE: For
stomachache, take
one tablet with a glass
of water as needed or
as directed by a
physician. Do not
exceed 6 tablets in
24 hours.

ⓓ

DIRECTIONS: Rub
HydraZone on dry
skin. Do not rub near
eyes.
IMPORTANT: If you
get HydraZone in
your eyes, wash
immediately with water.

1. Which one do you take after meals—a, b, c, or d?
2. Which one is for dry hands?
3. Which one do you take every four hours?
4. Which one is not for children?
5. Which one do you have to take with water?

6. You can't rub this one near your eyes. Which one is it?
7. You can't take this one more than four times a day. Which one is it?
8. Which one is good for most aches and pains?

Listen to the conversation and choose the correct answer.

1. The doctor's name is
   a. Carver.
   b. Carter.

2. The patient's name is
   a. Carver.
   b. Carter.

3. The patient has
   a. a bad cold.
   b. a bad toe.

4. The doctor can see the patient
   a. at 3:00 today.
   b. at 3:00 tomorrow.

5. The patient
   a. agrees to see the doctor today.
   b. wants to see the doctor tomorrow.

6. The doctor's office is at
   a. 1013 Johnson Street.
   b. 1030 Johnson Street.

Practice the conversation. Use the situations in the list.

1. You ate too much, and now you have a terrible stomachache.
2. There's something in your eye.
3. You have terrible chest pains.

4. You have a sore throat.
5. You hit your thumb, and now it's bleeding.
6. Your own idea.

A: Doctor's office. May I help you?
B: Yes. My name is _____. I'd like to make an appointment to see Dr. _____.
A: What seems to be the problem?
B: _____.
A: Well, Dr. _____ has an opening at _____. Can you come in then?
B: At _____? Yes, that would be fine.

> OR
> B: At _____? No, I'm sorry I can't. How about _____ morning/afternoon?
> A: Let's see. _____ morning/afternoon at _____?
> B: Yes, that would be fine.

A: All right. See you then.
B: Excuse me. What's your exact address?
A: _____.
B: Thank you.

Capitalize and punctuate Mrs. Young's note to her son's teacher. Use 3 commas (,), 3 periods (.), and 10 capital letters.

february 24 1992
dear miss brodsky
    alan is absent from class because he has a fever and a sore throat   he went to the doctor yesterday and he has to stay home and rest   please send him his homework
            sincerely
            joan young

Now write a note for a sick friend. Write the note to his or her teacher or boss.

Work with a group. Agree on one answer for each question. Report your answers to the class. Do your classmates agree?

1. What's the worst illness in the world?
2. What's the biggest country in the world?
3. What's the most intelligent animal?
4. What's the hardest language to learn?
5. Who's the most famous person in the world right now?
6. Write your own question.

REVIEW: THE COMPARATIVE OF ADJECTIVES

The selection at The Input is **smaller than** the selection at Computer World.

Computers at Computer World are **more expensive than** computers at Fast Frank's.

REVIEW: (NOT) AS . . . AS

Computer World is **as close as** Fast Frank's.

The salespeople at The Input are **not as friendly as** the salespeople at Computer World.

THE SUPERLATIVE OF ADJECTIVES

	the newest **the** nicest **the** biggest **the** busiest	
It is	**the most successful**	toy store in Dallas.
	the best **the worst**	
	the farthest	toy store from my house.

CLAUSES WITH *IF*: PRESENT TIME

What **do** you **do if** you **have** a toothache?
  I **go** to the dentist **if** I **have** a toothache.
  If you **have** a toothache, **take** two aspirin.

absent
adult
aspirin
bargain
car accident
complaint
computer game
dentist
directions
dosage
except
finance rate
if
illness
immediately
mile
opening
pain
pillow
problem
remedy
skin
solution
tablet
vitamin

as directed by a physician
as needed
daily/a day
every four hours
How about . . . ?
not to exceed . . .
See you then.
That would be fine.
What seems to be the problem?

VERBS
be close to
break [broke]
cut [cut]
drink [drank]
hurt [hurt]
lie down [lay]
return
rub [rubbed]
sell [sold]

ADJECTIVES

close
dry
exact
famous
high
honest
low
rude
soft
successful
wide

PARTS OF THE BODY

ankle
arm
back
cheek
chest
chin
ear
elbow
eye
finger
foot [feet]
forehead
hand
head
hip
knee
leg
mouth
neck
nose
shoulder
stomach
thumb
toe
tooth [teeth]
wrist

HEALTH PROBLEMS

a backache
a headache
a stomachache
a toothache
a runny nose
a sore throat
a cold
a cough
a fever
the flu

COMPARING

It is the busiest toy store around here.
It is the most successful toy store in Texas.

The selection at The Input is smaller than the selection at Computer World.
Computers at The Input are the cheapest.
The salespeople at The Input are not as friendly as the salespeople at Computer World.

COMPLAINING

I'd like to return these shoes.
    What's the problem with them?
They aren't comfortable at all.

ASKING FOR AND GIVING ADVICE

If you have a headache, take two aspirin.
What do you do if you have a backache?
    I lie down and rest if I have a backache.

MAKING SUGGESTIONS

Why don't you call a doctor?
    That's a good idea.
Why don't you look for a new job?
    That's a good suggestion.

GIVING OPINIONS

The flu is the worst illness in the world.
What's the most exciting sport?
    I think soccer is the most exciting sport.

MAKING A DOCTOR'S APPOINTMENT

I'd like to make an appointment to see Dr. Carter.
    He has an opening this afternoon at 3:00. Can you come in then?
Yes, that would be fine.
No, I'm sorry I can't. How about tomorrow afternoon?

TALKING ABOUT ILLNESS

What's the matter?
    I don't feel well.
    I hurt my arm.
    I broke my leg.
    I have a cold.
    I cut my finger.

OFFERING SYMPATHY

That's too bad.
I'm sorry to hear that.

Are you going to take a vacation?

Look at the picture. Then listen as you read the conversation.

Olga: Are you going to take a vacation this summer?

Lucy: No. Simon and I aren't going to go anywhere this year. We're going to stay home. What are you going to do?

Olga: We're going to go to Florida. We want to take the kids to Disney World.

Lucy: Oh, that's wonderful!

Olga: And from Florida we're going to fly to New York City!

Lucy: That's going to be a terrific vacation. I'm jealous.

Olga: Yes. I think we're going to have a great time. In fact, I just bought our tickets.

What's the answer to each question, *Lucy and her husband* or *Olga and her family*? Choose the correct one.

1. Who is going to take a vacation?
2. Who isn't going anywhere?
3. Who is going to stay home?
4. Who is going to go to Disney World and New York?

5. Who is going to have an exciting trip?
6. Who is going to have a quiet vacation at home?

Look at the examples below. Then complete the conversation between Olga and her travel agent.

Olga and her family **are going to take** a vacation this summer.
It **is going to be** a very exciting vacation.

Jack: Brown Travel. Jack Brown speaking.

Olga: Hello, Mr. Brown. This is Olga Delgado. I'm calling about my trip to Disney World and New York.

Jack: Oh, yes, Mrs. Delgado. You and your family (**1.** have) a wonderful time!

Olga: I know. I'm very excited.

Jack: Your plane (**2.** arrive) at 11:00 A.M. A guide (**3.** meet) you with a car at the airport, and she (**4.** take) you to Disney World.

Olga: Fine.

Jack: The guide knows Disney World very well, so she (**5.** show) you around.

Olga: All right.

Jack: Then at the end of the day, the car (**6.** take) you to your hotel.

Olga: And what are we going to do the next day?

Jack: The next morning you (**7.** meet) Mickey Mouse. He (**8.** introduce) your kids to his friends, and then he (**9.** go) with you to Tomorrowland.

Olga: It (**10.** be) a wonderful vacation, and the kids (**11.** love) it!

Jack: Yes, you (**12.** have) a terrific time.

Now listen to the conversation.

Look at the pictures and complete the conversations between Olga and Lucy.
Then listen to them. 📼

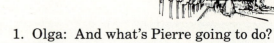

Olga: What's Oscar going to do for vacation?
Lucy: **He's going to go to** Spain. **He wants to** visit his family.

1. Olga: And what's Pierre going to do?
   Lucy: _____ France. _____ see the Eiffel Tower.

2. Olga: What's Pravit going to do?
   Lucy: _____ California. _____ visit his sister.

3. Olga: What are Mr. and Mrs. Brennan going to do?
   Lucy: _____ Japan. _____ climb Mt. Fuji.

4. Olga: What's Lynn going to do?
   Lucy: _____ Brazil. _____ take pictures of the famous beaches in Rio.

5. Olga: What are Gina and her parents going to do?
   Lucy: _____ Colorado. _____ ski in the mountains.

6. Olga: What's Tetsuo going to do?
   Lucy: _____ Hawaii. _____ relax in the sun all day.

What about you?
What are you going to do for vacation this year?

Look at the pictures and tell what happened very recently. 📼

Olga **just bought** five tickets to Florida. She and her family are going to take a vacation.

1. We (finish) exercise 3. It was very easy.

2. Jerry Brennan (buy) a gift for his wife. Her birthday is tomorrow.

3. We (see) *A Cowboy from Texas.* What an awful movie!

4. A: You (get) married, didn't you?
   B: No, but my brother did.

5. Roberto (call) his father. He calls him every week.

Complete the statements below. Use your imagination and the verbs in the list. You can make affirmative or negative sentences.

want (to)	hate (to)	have (to)	love (to)
like (to)	need (to)	'd like (to)	try (to)

Olga is going to take her family to Florida
  because they **like to** travel.
  because they **don't want to** stay in Dallas.
  because they **need** a rest.
  because they **try to** visit different places every year.

1. Roberto goes to bed early every night . . .
2. Ann and Jerry are going to buy a new car . . .
3. Pravit is going to a department store . . .
4. Oscar went to a travel agency yesterday . . .
5. Tetsuo just turned on the radio . . .
6. A lot of students go to the United States . . .

Try to guess the missing words. Then listen and check your guesses. 📼

A LOOK AT THE FUTURE

The houses of tomorrow are **1** _____ going to be the same
2 _____ they are today. They are **3** _____ to be very different.
They are going to **4** _____ computers and robots. The robots
5 _____ going to repair and clean the **6** _____. We are going
7 _____ connect our appliances and **8** _____ to computers. If
we leave our homes and forget to turn **9** _____ our stoves or
electric coffee pots, we **10** _____ going to call our computers
on the telephone and turn **11** _____ the appliances. **12** _____
we have to work late, we are going to **13** _____ our homes
and turn **14** _____ the lights.

Ticket, please.

Look at the picture. Then listen as you read the conversation. 📼

Tommy:	Mommy, are we going to fly on *that* plane?
Olga:	Yes, Tommy. We're going to fly on that plane.
Tommy:	Mommy, when are we going to get on the plane?
Olga:	We're going to get on the plane very soon.
Ticket Agent:	Ticket, please.
Olga:	Here you are.
Ticket Agent:	And where would you like to sit?
Olga:	Near the window.
Ticket Agent:	OK. You're in seats 5A, B, and C, and 6A and B.
Olga:	Thank you.
Ticket Agent:	You're welcome. Have a nice flight.

Practice the conversation.
Answer the questions with
your own information.

A: Ticket, please.
B: Here you are.
A: And where would you like to sit?
B: Near the window.
(On the aisle, please.)
A: Smoking or non-smoking?
B: Smoking.
(Non-smoking.)
A: OK. You're in seat _____.
B: Thank you.
A: You're welcome. Have a nice flight.

The Delgados are in the airport. First look at Olga's answers to Tommy's questions. Then complete their conversation. 📼

Tommy: Mommy, **are we going to fly** on *that* plane?
Olga: Yes, Tommy. We're going to fly on that plane.
Tommy: Mommy, **is the pilot going to let** me fly the plane?
Olga: No, the pilot isn't going to let you fly the plane.

Tommy: Mommy, ¹_____ lunch on the plane?
Olga: Yes, we are. We're going to have lunch on the plane.
Tommy: Well, ²_____ me where he sits?
Olga: Yes, the pilot's going to show you where he sits.
Tommy: And ³_____ a movie on our flight?
Olga: No, there isn't going to be a movie on our flight.
Tommy: ⁴_____ next to the window?
Olga: Yes, you are. You're going to sit next to the window.
Tommy: ⁵_____ soon?
Olga: No, we aren't going to get there soon.

The Delgados are on the plane now. Look at the examples and complete their conversation with *what, when, where,* or *how long.* 📼

Tommy: Daddy, **when are we going to arrive** in Florida?
Hector: We're going to arrive in about three hours.
Tommy: **How long are we going to stay** in Florida?
Hector: We're going to stay for three days.

Tommy: Then ¹_____?
Hector: We're going to go to New York City. But first you're going to see a lot of wonderful things at Disney World.
Tommy: ²_____ at Disney World?
Hector: You're going to see everything, and you're going to meet Mickey Mouse.
Tommy: ³_____ Mickey Mouse?
Hector: You're going to meet him tomorrow.
Tommy: You're closing your eyes. ⁴_____ do?
Hector: Your mother and I are going to sleep . . . and you are, TOO!

Look at the example below. Then ask and answer questions about the pictures.

> A: **Why** is Tony looking for Oscar's phone number?
> B: **Because** he's going to call Oscar.

1. A: Gina/walk to the post office
   B: Because/mail a letter

2. A: Oscar/open a bottle of juice
   B: Because/have a drink

3. A: Ann and Jerry/buy movie tickets
   B: Because/see a movie

4. A: Susan/turn off the lights
   B: Because/go to sleep

5. A: Pierre/go into a shoe store
   B: Because/buy some new shoes

Now listen to each exchange.

Listen and write the first eight lines of the conversation.

Man: 1 _____
Woman: 2 _____
Man: 3 _____
Woman: No. 4 _____
Man: 5 _____
Woman: 6 _____
Man: 7 _____
Woman: No. 8 _____
Man: Listen, I'm going to rent a car. Would you like a ride?
Woman: Oh, no thank you.
Man: Are you sure?
Woman: Yes. But thanks anyway.

Now practice the conversation. Use your own information.

Interview a classmate, a friend, or someone in your family. Find out . . .

1. when the person is going to take his or her next vacation.
2. where the person is going to go.
3. what the person is going to do there.
4. how long the person is going to stay there.
5. if the person is going to travel alone.
6. when the person is going to come back.
7. other information you want to know about the trip.

Arrivals and departures

You are at the airport with a friend. Look at the signs and ask and answer questions.

restaurant/
get something to eat

1. car rental area/
rent a car

2. newsstand/
buy a magazine

3. post office/
buy some stamps

> A: **Where are you going?**
> B: **I'm going** *to the restaurant.*
> **I'm going to** *get something to eat.*

4. baggage claim area/
get my suitcase

5. bank/
change some money

6. bus stop/
take a bus
into the city

Now give your own answers. Use your own ideas or the ideas in the list.

cash a traveler's check	get a newspaper	buy some stamps	buy some candy
take a bus to the hotel	mail a postcard	eat lunch	get a soda

Answer the questions about the flight arrivals and departures.

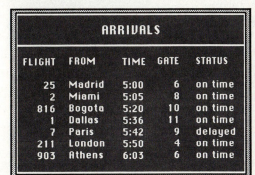

ARRIVALS				
FLIGHT	FROM	TIME	GATE	STATUS
25	Madrid	5:00	6	on time
2	Miami	5:05	8	on time
816	Bogota	5:20	10	on time
1	Dallas	5:36	11	on time
7	Paris	5:42	9	delayed
211	London	5:50	4	on time
903	Athens	6:03	6	on time

DEPARTURES				
FLIGHT	TO	TIME	GATE	STATUS
3	Tokyo	5:00	1	on time
14	Dallas	5:10	2	delayed
712	Boston	5:15	14	on time
33	Paris	5:36	8	on time
41	London	6:00	21	on time
52	Bogota	6:13	7	on time
9	Rome	6:40	10	on time

1. When is flight 25 from Madrid going to arrive?
2. When is flight 52 to Bogota going to depart?
3. Is flight 14 to Dallas going to leave on time?
4. What gate is flight 52 going to leave from?
5. What gate is flight 25 going to arrive at?

(continued)

Now ask and answer your own questions about the flight arrivals and departures.
Listen to the examples. 📼

A: When is *flight 25 from Madrid* **going to arrive?**
B: *At 5:00.*
A: Thank you.

A: Is *flight 14 to Dallas* **going to leave on time?**
B: *No, I'm sorry. It's delayed.*
A: Thanks.

EXERCISE 3

You are taking a boat trip around New York City, and you are listening to the guide. Complete the guide's description with the correct form and tense of the verbs (for example, live/lives, is/are living, lived, is/are going to live). Then listen to the guide. 📼

In front of us (**1.** be) the skyline of Manhattan. More than 3 million people (**2.** live) on that island, and more than 4 million people (**3.** work) there every day.

1. The skyline of Manhattan

Soon you (**4.** see) the Statue of Liberty in front of us. There she (**5.** be). Do you see her? Frederic Bartholdi (**6.** design) her and (**7.** begin) to build her in 1884. And on July 4, 1986, she (**8.** have) her 100th birthday! We (**9.** think) she's beautiful!

Right now our boat (**10.** move) by the World Trade Center, the tallest buildings in New York City. Each building (**11.** have) 110 floors, and sometimes the buildings (**12.** move) when the wind (**13.** blow).

2. The Statue of Liberty

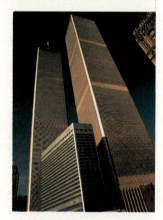

3. The World Trade Center

In five or ten minutes we (**14.** stop) at the South Street Seaport. Many years ago South Street (**15.** be) a busy port. Today it (**16.** be) a wonderful place to visit, shop, and eat. I (**17.** be) sure you (**18.** enjoy) your visit there.

4. The South Street Seaport

Listen to the questions about New York City. Choose the correct answers.

1. a. On an island.
   b. In New York City.
   c. Both a and b.

2. a. 3 million.
   b. 4 million.
   c. Guide didn't say.

3. a. 3 million.
   b. 4 million.
   c. Guide didn't say.

4. a. Bartholdi.
   b. In 1884.
   c. 100.

5. a. New York City.
   b. Bartholdi.
   c. Guide didn't say.

6. a. Yes.
   b. No.
   c. Guide didn't say.

7. a. Yes.
   b. No.
   c. Guide didn't say.

8. a. You can shop.
   b. You can eat.
   c. Both a and b.

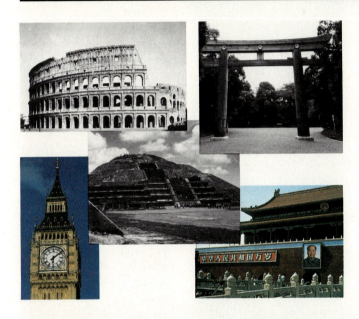

Work with a group and follow the directions.

1. First choose a city or place you all want to visit.
2. Decide when you are going to go and how you are going to get there.
3. Then make a list of the things you are going to do there.
4. Next, make a list of the things the people in your group are going to take on the trip.
5. Finally, tell the class about your group's future trip.

Capitalize and punctuate this postcard. Use 32 capital letters. Also use 3 commas (,), 6 periods (.), 2 question marks (?), and 2 apostrophes (').

Now write your own postcard. Pretend you and your classmates are on a trip in exercise 5 or on a different trip. Write what you are doing, what you did, and what you are going to do.

july 19

dear karen and paul
    we re in orlando and we re having a wonderful time yesterday we went to disney world and we saw all the sights we met mickey mouse too tomorrow we are going to sea world on thursday we are going to fly to new york
    how is everything in dallas are you enjoying a quiet vacation at home see you soon
                    sylvia and don

karen and paul smith
119 green street
dallas texas 75214

THE FUTURE WITH *BE GOING TO*

Affirmative and Negative Statements

I'm She's We're	(not) going to	take	a vacation this summer.

Yes/No Questions

Am I			
Is she	going to	fly	on that plane?
Are we			

Short Answers

Yes,	you **are**.
	she **is**.
	you **are**.

No,	you **aren't**.
	she **isn't**.
	you **aren't**.

Information (Wh-) Questions

When	am I is she are we	going to	arrive	in Florida?

THE IMMEDIATE PAST: *JUST*

Olga **just bought** five tickets to Florida.

REVIEW: VERB + *TO* + VERB

They	want to hate to love to like to try to would like to need to have to	travel	every year.

airport
aisle
anywhere
arrival
baggage claim
bar
boat
capital letter
car rental area
closing
Daddy
departure
electric
end
excited
famous
flight
gate
gift
greeting
guide
into
island
jealous
land (Tomorrowland)
million
Mommy
newsstand
pilot
portable
robot
seaport (port)
seat
sights
skyline
status
suitcase
sun
taxi stand
terrific
ticket agent
travel agency
traveler's check
wind

Thanks anyway.
Would you like a ride?

VOCABULARY

VERBS

blow [blew]
cash
connect
depart
design
fly [flew]
get [got] on
go [went] to sleep
introduce
let [let]
mail
repair
sign
ski
stop
turn off

PUNCTUATION

apostrophe (')
comma (,)
period (.)
question mark (?)

COMMUNICATION SUMMARY

TALKING ABOUT THE FUTURE

Are we going to fly on that plane?
    Yes, we're going to fly on that plane.
When are we going to arrive in Florida?
    We're going to arrive soon.

TALKING ABOUT THE PRESENT AND THE FUTURE

Where are you going?
    I'm going to the restaurant. I'm going to get something to eat.

TALKING ABOUT THE IMMEDIATE PAST

I just finished Unit 6.

GIVING REASONS

I'm studying English because I want to visit the United States.

TALKING ABOUT VACATIONS

When are you going to take your next vacation?
    In July.
Where are you going to go?
    I'm going to go to Spain.
How long are you going to stay?
    I'm going to stay two weeks.
Are you going to travel alone?
    Yes, I am.

CHECKING IN FOR A FLIGHT

Ticket, please.
    Here you are.
And where would you like to sit?
    Near the window, please.
Smoking or non-smoking?
    Non-smoking.
OK. You're in seat 5A.
    Thank you.
You're welcome. Have a nice flight.

ASKING FOR TRAVEL INFORMATION

Excuse me. When is flight 25 from Madrid going to arrive?
    At 5:00.
Is flight 14 to Dallas going to leave on time?
    No, I'm sorry. It's delayed.
What gate is flight 52 going to leave from?
    Gate 7.
What gate is flight 25 going to arrive at?
    Gate 6.

Can you tell me a little about yourself?

Look at the pictures. Then listen as you read the conversation.

Mr. Horn:	Miss Abe?
Keiko:	Yes.
Mr. Horn:	Please come in. I'm Bruce Horn, Director of Personnel.
Keiko:	I'm pleased to meet you.
Mr. Horn:	Please sit down.
Keiko:	Thank you.
Mr. Horn:	So, you want to be a secretary at United Bank. Can you tell me a little about yourself?
Keiko:	Well, I'm 19 years old. I was born in Japan, and I came here about a year ago. And I'm studying English and Business at school.
Mr. Horn:	You can speak English very well.
Keiko:	Thank you.
Mr. Horn:	Do you have any hobbies or special skills?
Keiko:	I like to read, and I like to swim.
Mr. Horn:	Can you use a computer?
Keiko:	No, I can't, but I'd like to learn about computers.
Mr. Horn:	But you can type, can't you?
Keiko:	Oh, yes. I can type about sixty words a minute.

Choose the correct answer.

1. Keiko is
   a. ninety.
   b. nine.
   c. nineteen.

2. She is studying
   a. Business.
   b. English.
   c. both a and b.

3. She came to the United States
   a. one year ago.
   b. nine years ago.
   c. nineteen years ago.

4. Keiko can
   a. use a computer.
   b. type.
   c. both a and b.

5. Keiko is trying to get a job
   a. in a factory.
   b. in a bank.
   c. at school.

6. Keiko types
   a. sixty words a minute.
   b. very well.
   c. both a and b.

Practice this conversation. Use your own information.

A: Can you tell me a little about yourself?
B: Well, I'm *19* years old. I was born in *Japan*, (*and I came here about a year ago*). And I'm studying *English* at school.
A: Do you have any hobbies?
B: I like to *read and swim*.

Complete the sentences with *can* or *can't (cannot)*.

Oscar **can play** tennis very well.

Oscar **can't ski** very well.

Oscar **can't swim at all**.

1. Lynn _____ take very good photographs.

2. Tony _____ dance very well.

3. Pravit _____ dance at all.

(continued)

4. Gina has the flu, so she _____ come to class tonight.

5. Lucy and Simon _____ sleep at night because their neighbors are very noisy.

6. Ann's car has a flat tire, but don't worry! Pravit _____ fix it.

What about you?
I can _____ very well.
I can't _____ very well/ at all.

7. It's raining. They _____ play baseball.

8. I'm sorry. I _____ do this. It's very difficult.

EXERCISE 4

Listen and choose the letter of the words you hear. 📼

1. a. We can ski . . .
   b. We can't ski . . .

2. a. Tetsuo can play the guitar . . .
   b. Tetsuo can't play the guitar . . .

3. a. Gina can go to the party . . .
   b. Gina can't go to the party . . .

4. a. A lot of students can type . . .
   b. A lot of students can't type . . .

5. a. Lynn can take our pictures today . . .
   b. Lynn can't take our pictures today . . .

6. a. We can walk there . . .
   b. We can't walk there . . .

7. a. He can speak English very well . . .
   b. He can't speak English very well . . .

8. a. I can help you with your homework . . .
   b. I can't help you with your homework . . .

Now complete the sentences above with the endings in the list.

a. because it's very far and it's going to rain.
b. and we can play tennis.
c. but he can play the piano very well.
d. because I don't understand it.

e. because she's sick.
f. but she can take them tomorrow.
g. and use computers.
h. so he doesn't study very much.

Look at the examples. Then ask and answer questions about the pictures. Use the verbs in the list. 🔲

fix   bake   speak   drive   use   type   file   change

A: Can she **drive** a truck?
B: Yes, she **can.**

A: Can she **type** well?
B: No, she **can't.**

1. A: _____ English?
   B: _____ .

2. A: _____ good cakes?
   B: _____ .

3. A: _____ washing
      machines?
   B: _____ .

4. A: _____ well?
   B: _____ .

What about your partner?
A: Can you _____?
B: Yes, I can./
   No, I can't.

5. A: _____ flat tires?
   B: _____ .

6. A: _____ photocopy
      machine?
   B: _____ .

Do your classmates agree with your answers in exercise 5? Find out. Follow the examples. 🔲

A: She can drive a truck, **can't** she?
B: Yes, she can.

A: She can't type well, **can** she?
B: No, she can't.

We've got to do something!

Look at the pictures. Then listen as you read the conversation.

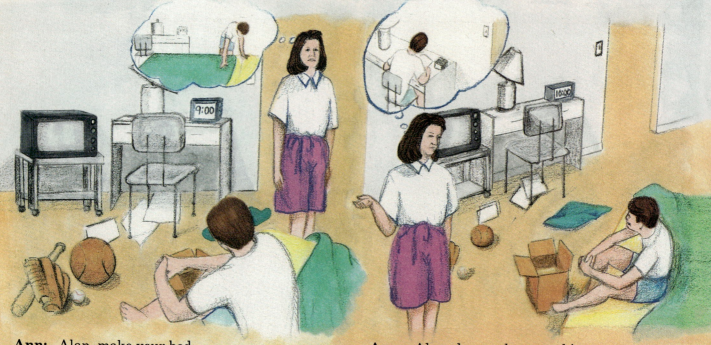

Ann: Alan, make your bed.
Alan: Yeah. OK. In just a minute.

Ann: Alan, do your homework!
Alan: Oh, Mom, do I have to? It's Saturday!
Ann: Yes, you have to.
Alan: But I can't do my homework now. I have to make my bed first.

Ann: Alan, could you help me in the kitchen?
Alan: In a minute, Mom. I want to watch the end of this.

Ann: Jerry, we've got to do something! Alan never listens. He never does anything. He only watches television.
Jerry: I agree. He's got to do his homework, and he's got to help around the house.

Look at the example and continue the conversation between Alan and his mother. Then listen to each exchange.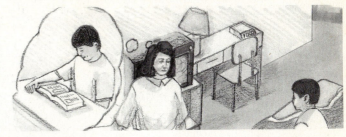

> **Ann:** *Do your homework!*
> **Alan:** **Do I have to?**
> **Ann:** **Yes, you have to. (Yes, you do.)**
> **Alan:** **But I can't** *do my homework* **now. I have to** *make my bed* **first.**

1. Ann: (walk the dog)
   Alan: (do my homework)

2. Ann: (take out the garbage)
   Alan: (walk the dog)

3. Ann: (clean your room)
   Alan: (take out the garbage)

4. Ann: (feed the cat)
   Alan: (clean my room)

5. Ann: (finish your homework)
   Alan: (feed the cat)

Practice inviting and giving excuses as in the example. Then listen to each exchange.

> **A: Do you want to** *go to the movies with me tonight?*
> OR
> **Would you like to** *go to the movies with me tonight?*
> **B: I'm sorry, I can't. I** *have to wash my hair.*

1. A: (go to the opera on Saturday night)
   B: (have to study)

2. A: (go to the beach this weekend)
   B: (have to paint my house)

3. A: (get a cup of coffee after class)
   B: (have to go home and feed my cat)

4. A: (take a ride in my new car)
   B: (be busy right now)

Say these questions and answers a different way. Use *could* in your questions. Use *'ve got (have got)* and *'s got (has got)* in your answers. Then listen to each exchange.

A: Can you help me in the kitchen, please?
B: I can't right now. I **have to** study.

A: Could you help me in the kitchen, please?
B: I can't right now. I**'ve got to** study.

A: Can Lynn take my picture now?
B: She can't right now. She **has to** go home.

A: Could Lynn take my picture now?
B: She can't right now. She**'s got to** go home.

1. A: Can you erase the board for me?
   B: I can't right now. I have to go home.

2. A: Can Alan come outside and play?
   B: He can't go out right now. He has to finish his homework.

3. A: Can you tell me the answers?
   B: We can't tell you right now. We have to finish the exercise first.

4. A: Can I have a piece of cake, please?
   B: You can't have one right now. You have to wait until dinner.

5. A: Can your friends go to the concert?
   B: They can't go to the concert. They have to go to work.

6. A: Make your own request.
   B: Give your own reason or excuse.

Listen and complete the conversation.

Man: Would you like to go to a movie tonight?
Keiko: Oh, ¹_____. ²_____. ³_____.
Man: Oh, do you go to school?
Keiko: Yes. ⁴_____.
Man: That's interesting. Well, do you want to go to the beach on Saturday?
Keiko: No, ⁵_____. ⁶_____.
Man: Well, could I have your telephone number so I can call you sometime?
Keiko: No, ⁷_____.
Man: I see. Well, nice talking to you.
Keiko: ⁸_____.

Now practice making and refusing invitations. Use your own information and practice the conversation above.

Help wanted

First look up the words you don't know in your dictionary. Next, match the words and the abbreviations.

1. Salary	c	8. Necessary	___
2. Experience	___	9. Full time	___
3. Appointment	___	10. Part time	___
4. High school graduate	___	11. And	___
5. Good	___	12. Benefits	___
6. Hours	___	13. Typing	___
7. Excellent	___	14. Available	___

a. **Typ.**
b. HS Grad.
c. **Sal.**
d. **FT**
e. **Hrs.**
f. Exp.
g. **Bnfts.**

n. *Avail.*
i. *Appt.*
j. PT
k. Nec.
l. **&**
m. *Excel.*
n. *Gd.*

Read the employment ads. Then match the description with the job.

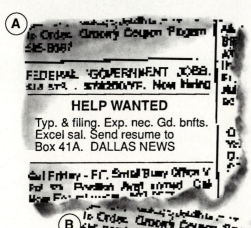

1. You have to type. JOB **A**
2. You can work full time or part time. JOB ___
3. You need previous experience. JOB ___
4. You have to be a high school graduate. JOB ___
5. There are good benefits. JOB ___
6. The salary is very good. JOB ___
7. You can begin work today. JOB ___
8. You can't call to apply for this job. JOB ___
9. You need a resume. JOB ___
10. You have to call during the day. JOB ___
11. The job is in a restaurant. JOB ___

Listen to the job interview. Then complete these notes.

> *Applicant's years of exp:*
> *Reason for leaving last job:*
> *Reason for wanting this job: The people are nice and the restaurant is very good.*
> *Position:*
> *Sal:*
> *Hrs:*
> *Bnfts: There's health insurance, one sick day a month, and two weeks vacation.*

EXERCISE 4

Work with a partner and pretend one of you is interviewing for a job. Choose one of the jobs in exercise 2 or a job you would like to have. Ask and answer these job interview questions.

A: Which job would you like to apply for?
B: _____.
A: How many years of experience do you have in this kind of work?
B: _____.
A: Where did you work before?
B: _____.
A: Why did you leave your last job? (Why do you want to leave your present job?)
B: _____.
A: Why do you want to work here?
B: _____.

A: Do you have any questions you'd like to ask me?
B: Yes. What's the salary?
A: _____.
B: What are the hours?
A: _____.
B: What are the benefits?
A: _____.
B: How many sick days are there?
A: _____.
B: How much vacation time is there?
A: _____.

Read Ann Brennan's resume.
Then write your own resume.

ANN BRENNAN
674 Vincent Drive
Dallas, Texas 75201
(214) 555-2499

EDUCATION:

1981 - 1983	MA, English New York University
1977 - 1981	BA, Spanish Texas State University
1974 - 1977	Grover Cleveland High School El Paso, Texas

EMPLOYMENT:

| 1983 - Present | English Teacher
The Language Institute, Dallas, Texas
Teach classes at all levels |
| 1981 - 1983 | Saleswoman
Brenton's Bookstore, New York, New York
Worked evenings and weekends |

SKILLS: Type
Speak, read, and write Spanish and French

NAME
_____

ADDRESS
_____
TELEPHONE

EDUCATION:

DATES	DEGREE
	LAST SCHOOL (OR PRESENT SCHOOL)
	PREVIOUS SCHOOL (IF ANY)

EMPLOYMENT:

DATES	PRESENT OR LAST JOB AND DESCRIPTION
	PREVIOUS JOB AND DESCRIPTION

SKILLS:

GRAMMAR SUMMARY

CAN

Affirmative Statements

I You He She (It) We They	**can**	**play**	tennis very well.

Negative Statements

I You He She (It) We They	**can't (cannot)**	**ski**	very well.

Yes/No Questions

Can	I you he she (it) we they	**type?**

Short Answers

Yes,	I you he she (it) we they	**can.**
No,		**can't.**

Tag Questions

She can drive a truck,	**can't she?**
But she can't ride a bicycle,	**can she?**

Yes, she can. No, she can't.

REVIEW: *HAVE (HAS) TO*

Statements

I **have to make** my bed.
She **has to go.**

Yes/No Questions

Do I **have to do** my homework?
  Yes, you **have to.** (Yes, you **do.**)

HAVE (HAS) GOT TO

I	**'ve (have)**		
He She	**'s (has)**	**got to**	**study.**
We You They	**'ve (have)**		

REVIEW: *AND, BUT, BECAUSE, AND SO*

We can ski **and** we can play tennis.
Tetsuo can't play the guitar, **but** he plays the piano very well.
Gina can't go to the party **because** she's sick.
He can speak English very well **so** he doesn't study very much.

VOCABULARY

a little
applicant
available
below
benefits
college
description
education
elementary school
employment
excuse
experience
filing
flat tire
full time
graduate
guitar
health insurance
high school
industry
institute
invitation
language
level
necessary
noisy
opera
outside
part time
photocopy machine
plus
position

VOCABULARY

previous
request
resume
sometime
tips
truck
truth
typing
washing machine
yourself

B.A. (Bachelor of Arts)
Director of Personnel
Nice talking to you.
M.A. (Master of Arts)

VERBS

apply for
desire
erase
feed [fed] my cat
graduate
interview
make [made] my bed
rain
send [sent]
sleep [slept]
take [took] a ride
take out the garbage
wait
walk the dog

COMMUNICATION SUMMARY

ASKING FOR AND GIVING PERSONAL INFORMATION

Can you tell me a little about yourself?
    I'm 19 years old.
    I was born in Japan.
    I'm studying English at school.
    I like to read, and I like to swim.

TALKING ABOUT ABILITY

I can ski very well.
I can't swim at all.

Can he type?
    Yes, he can.
Can she use a computer?
    No, she can't.

ASKING FOR CONFIRMATION

She can swim, can't she?
    Yes, she can.
She can't type, can she?
    No, she can't.

GIVING REASONS OR EXCUSES

I can't do my homework now. I have to make my bed.

INVITING AND REFUSING INVITATIONS

Do you want to go to the movies with me tonight?
    I'm sorry, I can't. I have to wash my hair.
Would you like to go to the opera Saturday night?
    I'm sorry, I can't. I have to study.

MAKING REQUESTS

Could you help me in the kitchen, please?
    I can't right now. I've got to study.
Can Lynn take my picture now, please?
    She can't right now. She's got to go home.

Will you marry me?

Look at the pictures. Then listen as you read the conversation.

Gina: Lynn, can you keep a secret?
Lynn: Sure. What is it?
Gina: Promise you won't tell anyone?
Lynn: I promise. What is it?
Gina: Frank asked me to *marry* him!
Lynn: You're kidding! What did you say?
Gina: I didn't say anything. I don't know what to do.
Lynn: Why don't you talk to Madam Suzanne?
Gina: Who's that?
Lynn: She's a fortuneteller. She'll tell you about your future.
Gina: Oh, I don't believe in fortunetellers.
Lynn: A lot of people don't, but sometimes the information is interesting.
Gina: Hmmm. Will she tell me about my life with Frank?
Lynn: I'm sure she will. She's very good.

Read the conversation on page 86 again. Then answer *That's right, That's wrong,* or *It doesn't say.*

1. Frank wants to marry Gina.
2. Gina wants to marry Frank.
3. Madam Suzanne tells people about their future.

4. Lynn likes Madam Suzanne.
5. Gina likes Madam Suzanne.
6. Lynn won't tell Gina's secret.

What does Frank promise Gina? Complete the sentences with *'ll (will)* or *won't (will not).*

> I'll **be** a good husband.
> I **won't disappoint** you.

1. We _____ have a wonderful life.
2. You _____ never be unhappy.

3. I _____ bring you flowers every day.
4. I _____ fix things around the house.
5. We _____ visit your mother every month.
6. I _____ leave my dirty clothes on the floor.
7. I _____ complain about your cooking.
8. I _____ forget your birthday.

What does Madam Suzanne tell Gina? Complete the sentences with the future tense of the verbs in parentheses.

1. Your husband (be) a tall man with blond hair.
2. Your parents (not like) your husband.
3. You (live) in a big house.
4. Your husband (not be) neat.
5. You (have) six children.
6. You (meet) a lot of interesting people.
7. You (travel).
8. Your husband (not remember) your birthday.
9. Your husband (love) you.
10. That (be) five dollars.

Now answer these questions.

11. What does Frank really look like?
12. Are fortunetellers always right?

Gina's parents are talking. What are Mr. Poggi's questions? Look at the example.

> Gina/marry Frank
>
> Mr. Poggi: **Will** Gina **marry** Frank?
> Mrs. Poggi: Yes, I think she will.

1. they/be happy
   Mr. Poggi: _____?
   Mrs. Poggi: Yes, they will.

2. he/buy a house for her
   Mr. Poggi: _____?
   Mrs. Poggi: Yes, he will.

3. they/live near us
   Mr. Poggi: _____?
   Mrs. Poggi: No, they won't.

4. Gina/quit her job
   Mr. Poggi: _____?
   Mrs. Poggi: No, I don't think she will.

5. Frank/be a good father
   Mr. Poggi: _____?
   Mrs. Poggi: Yes, I think he will.

Now listen to each exchange. 🔲

Listen and complete Lynn's part of the conversation. 🔲

Lynn: Well, ¹_____?
Gina: I don't know.
Lynn: ²_____?
Gina: Yes, I will.
Lynn: ³_____?
Gina: I think that he will. I know he loves me.
Lynn: And ⁴_____?
Gina: Yes. I love him very much.

Lynn: ⁵_____?
Gina: No, they won't. That's the problem. They don't like him very much.
Lynn: Well, ⁶_____?
Gina: I don't know.
Lynn: Well, ⁷_____.
Gina: Yes, he's very patient, but I'll tell him very soon.

Frank is talking to his father. Complete Frank's promises. Then listen to each exchange. 🔲

> Mr. Russo: Make Gina happy.   Mr. Russo: Don't be messy.
> Frank: Don't worry. **I will.**   Frank: I promise **I won't.**

1. Mr. Russo: Help around the house.
   Frank: Don't worry. _____.

2. Mr. Russo: Be nice to her parents.
   Frank: OK. _____.

3. Mr. Russo: Don't forget her birthday.
   Frank: I promise that _____.

4. Mr. Russo: Don't complain.
   Frank: All right. _____.

5. Mr. Russo: Don't watch TV all the time.
   Frank: Don't worry. _____.

6. A: Tell your partner to do something.
   B: I promise (that) _____.
   All right/OK/don't worry. _____.

A long and healthy life

Look at the illustration. Then listen as you read the information. 📼

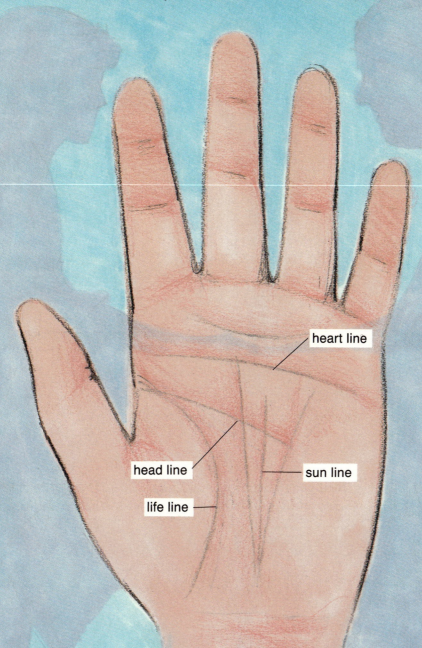

heart line

head line

sun line

life line

If you have a long and strong life line,
you'll have a long and healthy life.

If there aren't any breaks in your life line,
you'll have an easy life.

If two branches move up and away from your life line,
you won't have any money problems.

Look at the example and complete the sentences.

If you **have** a long life line, you'll **have** a long and healthy life.

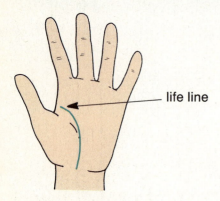

life line

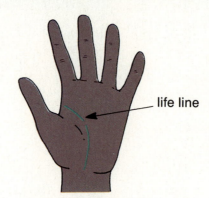

life line

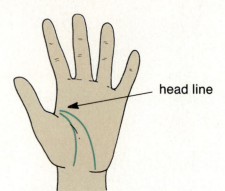

head line

1. If your life line (turn) down, you (travel) a lot.

2. If there (be) a break in the life line, there (be) a big change in your life.

3. If your head line and your life line (begin) together, you (not be) lonely.

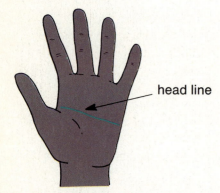

head line

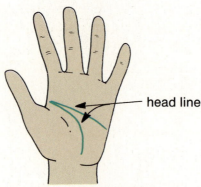

head line

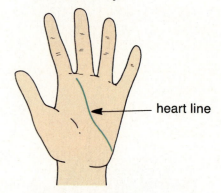

heart line

4. If your head line (go) straight across your hand, you (do) well in school.

5. If you (have) two head lines, you (do) well in business.

6. If your heart line (look) long and straight, you (not get) sick very often.

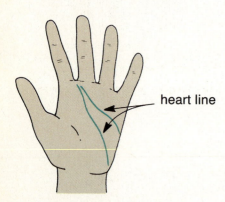

heart line

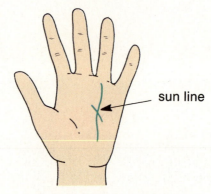

sun line

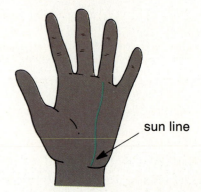

sun line

7. If you (have) two heart lines, you (make) a good husband or wife.

8. If any small lines (cross) your sun line, you (earn) a lot of money.

9. If your sun line (begin) near the bottom of your hand, you (be) famous.

Complete Gina's thoughts about marrying Frank. Look at the example.

> Madam Suzanne said we'll have six children. **If we have** six children, I **won't be** very happy.
>
> OR
>
> I **won't be** very happy **if** we **have** six children.

1. Madam Suzanne said my parents won't like my husband. I (not be) happy if they (not like) him.
2. She said we'll live in a big house. If we (live) in a big house, I (have to) clean all the time.
3. She said we'll travel. If we (travel), I (be) very happy.
4. She said we'll meet a lot of interesting people. We (have) a good time if we (meet) a lot of interesting people.
5. She said I'll marry a tall man with blond hair. If I marry a tall man with blond hair, it (not be) Frank!
6. Madam Suzanne can't be right! If I (not marry) Frank, I (not marry) anybody!

Frank is talking to his mother. Complete the questions with the words from the list.

What	when	how long	why	how
what time	what kind of wedding			where

Mrs. Russo: ¹_____ will you do if Gina says no?
Frank: I don't know.
Mrs. Russo: ²_____ will she give you an answer?
Frank: I'm sure she'll give me an answer soon.
Mrs. Russo: ³_____ will you wait?
Frank: I'm very patient. I'll wait a long time.
Mrs. Russo: ⁴_____ will you live if you get married?
Frank: We'll probably buy a house near school.
Mrs. Russo: ⁵_____ will you live there?
Frank: Because Gina has class at night and we don't have a car.
Mrs. Russo: ⁶_____ will you pay for a house?
Frank: Well, I have a good job, and Gina works, too.
Mrs. Russo: ⁷_____ will you have?
Frank: A small one. We'll invite our families and a few friends.
Mrs. Russo: ⁸_____ will you get married?
Frank: I don't know yet. Gina wants to get married at 2 o'clock, but I want a morning wedding.

Now listen to the conversation.

Complete these sentences with your own ideas. Look at the example.

> **If class ends early today,** *I'll probably go to a movie.*
> *We won't have class tomorrow* **if the teacher is sick.**

1. _____, I'll take an umbrella to school.
2. If we don't have much homework today, _____.
3. If I can't take the next English class, _____.
4. Make your own sentence.

First, read the article and try to guess the missing words. Then listen and check your guesses.

FORTUNETELLERS

Many people around the world [1] _____ to fortunetellers. These people think that fortunetellers will tell [2] _____ about their futures. There are [3] _____ kinds of fortunetellers, and they [4] _____ different ways to tell the [5] _____.

The study of palms began several centuries ago in India. Palm readers study the lines and sizes of people's hands to tell the future. Palm readers say that every line has a name and a meaning. A strong head line, for example, means a person is intelligent.

Numerology started in China. It [6] _____ the study of numbers. Numerologists use people's names and birth [7] _____ to explain their personalities and to tell about their pasts and their [8] _____. They give each letter of [9] _____ alphabet a number from one [10] _____ nine. Then they add together the [11] _____ in a person's name and [12] _____ date to get information about that person.

Graphology is the study of handwriting. Graphologists think the way people write gives information about their personalities. For example, if you write with lines that go up, you'll have a happy life, but if you write with lines that go down, you won't.

Other fortunetellers read cards or tea leaves. Some study the size [13] _____ clouds and watch the stars [14] _____ the moon. In any case, [15] _____ have one thing in common: [16] _____ tell us about the future. However, can they really do this? And, more important, do we really want to know the future?

Work in a group and answer these questions. Use the information in the article in exercise 5 and your own ideas.

1. Why do people go to fortunetellers?
2. Name three different kinds of fortunetellers. In what ways are they the same? In what ways are they different?
3. Gina went to a fortuneteller to talk about marrying Frank. Is this a good way to make an important decision? Why?
4. Some companies use graphology to decide which people they want to hire. Why?
5. Some states in the United States have laws against fortunetellers. Do you think fortunetellers are dangerous?
6. Did you or someone you know ever see a fortuneteller? What did the fortuneteller say? Was the fortuneteller right?

What sign are you?

Not everybody believes in horoscopes, but some people do. Read the horoscopes below. Then choose the correct answers on page 94.

YOUR HOROSCOPE

ARIES: MARCH 21 - APRIL 19

You are a good leader. People listen to you. You have a lot of energy, and you aren't afraid. You sometimes let other people finish your work.

TAURUS: APRIL 20 - MAY 20

Love is important to you. You will be a good husband or wife. You will make your home beautiful. You make people comfortable.

GEMINI: MAY 21 - JUNE 20

You have two personalities: Sometimes you are optimistic and think everthing is wonderful; sometimes you are pessimistic and think life isn't very good. You are very intelligent. You can think quickly and do many things. You have a good sense of humor.

CANCER: JUNE 21 - JULY 22

Sometimes you are happy, sometimes you are sad. Your home and family are very important to you. You like them better than business. You like to think about the past.

LEO: JULY 23 - AUGUST 22

You are a leader. You always say what you think. You are comfortable when you are the boss. You like to help other people.

VIRGO: AUGUST 23 - SEPTEMBER 22

You are very intelligent. You are quiet, you work hard, and people like you. You enjoy your job and want other people to work as hard as you do.

LIBRA: SEPTEMBER 23 - OCTOBER 22

You will be a good partner in marriage and business. You are very intelligent and a good listener. You understand problems and take care of them easily.

SCORPIO: OCTOBER 23 - NOVEMBER 21

You have a strong personality and you like to be the boss, but sometimes you aren't very sensitive to other people. You can do many things well, and you work very hard. You want other people to work hard, too.

SAGITTARIUS: NOVEMBER 22 - DECEMBER 21

You have a lot of energy and you are always busy. You like sports and things you can do outdoors. You are very healthy and you usually work very hard. You like to laugh and you enjoy life, but you worry a lot.

CAPRICORN: DECEMBER 22 - JANUARY 19

You always tell people what you think. You are seldom happy with things you have and you always want something else. Sometimes you make other people sad. You think you are smarter than other people. You are very good at business.

AQUARIUS: JANUARY 20 - FEBRUARY 18

You love other people and you have a lot of friends. You see the good side of everything. You can do a lot in a short time. You are very healthy.

PISCES: FEBRUARY 19 - MARCH 20

You are very sensitive, and you worry about what people think about you. You have a happy personality. You are friendly and easy to be with. You have a lot of friends. You don't always know what you want.

Choose the correct answers.

1. If you are a good leader (Aries),
   a. people listen to you.
   b. people do what you want.
   c. both a and b.

2. If you have two personalities (Gemini),
   a. you think and do things differently at different times or on different days.
   b. you have a twin.
   c. both a and b.

3. Optimistic (Gemini) means
   a. you don't think life is very good.
   b. you think life is good.
   c. neither a nor b.

4. Pessimistic (Gemini) means
   a. you don't think life is very good.
   b. you think life is good.
   c. neither a nor b.

5. If you have a strong personality (Scorpio),
   a. you want to be the leader.
   b. you always think you are right and want to do things your way.
   c. both a and b.

6. If you have a lot of energy (Sagittarius),
   a. you like to play sports, work hard, and do things around the house.
   b. you like to rest, read, or watch television.
   c. neither a nor b.

7. You are very sensitive (Scorpio and Pisces) means
   a. you show your feelings easily.
   b. you don't show your feelings easily.
   c. both a and b.

8. Seldom (Capricorn) means
   a. always.
   b. not very often.
   c. neither a nor b.

EXERCISE 2

Pretend you believe in horoscopes. Talk about people's signs. Listen to the examples.

A: **What sign are you?**
B: *Cancer.*
A: **Then** *your home and family are very important to you.*
B: **Yes. (I don't really know much about people's signs/horoscopes.)**

You have two personalities: Sometimes you are optimistic and think everthing is wonderful; sometimes you are pessimistic and think life isn't very good. You are very intelligent. You can think quickly and do many things. You have a good sense of humor.

CANCER: JUNE 21 - JULY 22
Sometimes you are happy, sometimes you are sad. Your home and family are very important to you. You like them better than business. You like to think about the past.

LEO: JULY 23 - AUGUST 22
You are a leader. You always say what you think. You are comfortable when you are the boss. You like to help other people.

VIRGO: AUGUST 23 - SEPTEMBER 22
You are very intelligent. You are quiet, you

Tom and his friend Bob are talking about Tom's fiancee Rosa. Listen and choose the best answers. 🔲

1. Tom
   a. wants to get married.
   b. isn't sure he wants to get married.

2. Tom's fiancee Rosa
   a. wants to get married.
   b. isn't sure she wants to get married.

3. Rosa will give Tom an answer
   a. on Saturday.
   b. on Sunday.

4. Tom
   a. thinks Rosa is a Pisces.
   b. doesn't know Rosa's sign.

5. If they have children,
   a. Tom wants Rosa to quit her job.
   b. Tom doesn't want Rosa to quit her job.

6. Bob is going fishing
   a. with his father on Saturday.
   b. with his girlfriend on Sunday.

7. Bob will get home
   a. around 7 o'clock.
   b. around 8 o'clock.

8. On Sunday, Bob and his girlfriend
   a. will probably go to a movie alone.
   b. will probably go to a movie with Tom and Rosa.

EXERCISE 4

Look at the things Tom will do. Then complete the chart with the things you and two classmates will do.

THINGS WE'LL (PROBABLY) DO		
This Week	*This Month*	*This Year*
Tom will have a date with his fiancee.	He'll work a lot.	He'll probably get married.
You . . .		
Classmate . . .		
Classmate . . .		

EXERCISE 5

Read Rosa's note. One sentence doesn't fit well in the note because it isn't necessary information. Which one is it?

Linda —
I won't be in class tomorrow. I'm going to go fishing with Tom. He has a day off so I'm going to take a day off, too. There's going to be a big sale at Whiteman's Department Store tomorrow. Will you please call me tomorrow night and tell me the homework assignment? I'll probably be home around 6:00. I'll talk to you then.
Thanks.
Rosa

Now write your own note.

1. Tell a classmate you are going to take a day off.
2. Say what you are going to do.
3. Ask your classmate to call with the homework assignment.
4. Say when you'll return.
5. Give only necessary information.

THE FUTURE WITH WILL

Affirmative and Negative Statements

I You He She It We They	'll (will) won't (will not)	disappoint	you.

Yes/No Questions

Will	I you he she it we they	be	happy?

Short Answers

Yes,	you I/we he	will.
No,	she it we/you they	won't.

Information (Wh-) Questions

When	will	you he she we they	get married?

REVIEW: CONJUNCTION THAT

I think (**that**) she will.
I promise (**that**) I will.

THE CONDITIONAL WITH IF . . . WILL (POSSIBLE SITUATIONS)

If	class	ends	early today,	I	'll probably go	to a movie.
If	the teacher	is	sick,	we	won't have	class tomorrow.

I'll probably go	to a movie	if	class	ends	early today.
We won't have	class tomorrow	if	the teacher	is	sick.

VOCABULARY

a few
against
away
boss
bottom
branch
card
century
cloud
cooking
decision
down
easily
energy
feelings
fiancee/fiance
fishing
fortuneteller
graphologist
graphology
handwriting
holiday
horoscope
law
leader
listener
marriage
meaning
messy
necessary
numerologist
numerology
optimistic
outdoors
palm
patient
personality
pessimistic
president
reader
seldom
sensitive
several
side

VOCABULARY

sign
smart
straight
tea leaves
up
way
wedding

Can you keep a secret?
In any case,
neither . . . nor . . .
one thing in common
Promise you won't tell
   anyone.
You're kidding!

VERBS

be afraid
believe (in)
complain (about)
cross
disappoint
earn
explain
have a date (with)
laugh
marry
pay [paid] attention (to)
promise
quit [quit]
win [won]
worry

SUN SIGNS

Aquarius
Aries
Cancer
Capricorn
Gemini
Leo
Libra
Pisces
Sagittarius
Scorpio
Taurus
Virgo

COMMUNICATION SUMMARY

TALKING ABOUT THE FUTURE

If you have a long and strong lifeline, you'll have a long and
healthy life.
We won't have class tomorrow if the teacher is sick.
Are you going to marry Frank?
   I don't know.
Will you decide soon?
   Yes, I will.
What will you do if Gina says no?
   I don't know.

MAKING PREDICTIONS

Your husband will be a tall man with blond hair.
You'll have six children.

TALKING ABOUT PROBABILITY

Tom will probably get married.
They will probably go to a movie on Sunday.

MAKING PROMISES

I'll be a good husband.
I won't disappoint you.
Don't be messy.
   I promise I won't.
Help around the house.
   I will.
Don't forget your wife's birthday.
   Don't worry. I won't.

TALKING ABOUT HOROSCOPES

What sign are you?
   Cancer.
Then your home and family are very important to you.

Which one should I buy?

Look at the picture. Then listen as you read the conversation. 🔲

Gina: Susan, please. Make up your mind. I'm exhausted.

Susan: I know, I'm tired, too. But this is an important decision. Oh, which one should I buy?

Yon Mi: Susan, you're young! Why don't you buy a sports car? Sports cars are fun.

Susan: Maybe you're right. The red one is nice. Maybe I'll look at that one.

Lucy: Wait a minute! You won't be single forever, you know. You should think about the future and buy a family car.

Susan: Hmm. That's good advice, too. Oh, I'm confused. I don't know what to do.

Gina: What about that green car? It's a lot bigger, and it isn't too expensive.

Susan: Oh, I don't know. The red sports car is nice, but you're right, Lucy. It's too small and impractical. And I really can't afford it. I think I'll buy the green one.

Yon Mi: Well, it's your choice, but you shouldn't decide too quickly. Let's go get a cup of coffee. We can sit and talk about it and come back later.

Susan: Good idea!

Choose the sentences that describe Susan.

1. a. She's tired.
   b. She has a lot of energy.

2. a. She's young.
   b. She's old.

3. a. She's single.
   b. She's married.

4. a. She's confused.
   b. She knows what she wants.

5. a. She's practical.
   b. She's impractical.

6. a. She can afford an expensive car.
   b. She can't afford an expensive car.

EXERCISE 2

Listen and complete the conversation with *should* or *shouldn't (should not)*.

Salesman: Do you like this sports car?

Susan: Oh, yes. But it's too expensive. I can't afford it.

Salesman: You're young. You ¹_____ have fun. Are you married?

Susan: No.

Salesman: Then you ²_____ buy a family car right now.

Susan: I know, but I'm very practical. I ³_____ buy a car I can use in the future.

Salesman: You're confused, aren't you?

Susan: Yes. So I really ⁴_____ make a decision right now.

Salesman: I agree. You ⁵_____ think about it.

Susan: Well, I think my friends are tired. We ⁶_____ take a break. Thank you for your help.

Salesman: You're welcome.

EXERCISE 3

What should or shouldn't Susan do? Match each sentence on the left with the best response.

1. Susan likes to drive fast. _____
2. She thinks big cars are safer than small cars. _____
3. She likes to listen to music. _____
4. Gas is expensive. _____
5. Dallas is very hot in the summer. _____
6. She can't afford an expensive car. _____
7. She isn't a very good driver. _____
8. She has to drive her aunt and uncle to work. _____

a. She shouldn't get a two-door car.
b. She should buy an economical car.
c. She shouldn't buy an expensive foreign car.
d. She should get a car with air conditioning.
e. She should get a sports car.
f. She shouldn't get a small car.
g. She should get a car with a good radio.
h. She should practice a lot.

Now combine each pair of sentences above into *one* sentence. Look at the example.

Susan likes to drive fast **so** she should get a sports car.

Work with a group. Give advice with *should* or *shouldn't*. Look at the example.

Roberto is parking next to a NO PARKING sign.

1. Pierre is at a gas station. He is smoking.

2. Pravit is going to drive to work. He left his wallet on the kitchen table.

> He **should move** his car.
> He **shouldn't park** his car there.

3. Lynn broke her glasses yesterday. She can't see well without them.

4. Tony is driving very fast, and there's a police car behind him.

5. Gina's tire is flat.

Ask and answer questions as in the examples.

> you / wear a seat belt when you drive
> A: **Should** *you* **wear** *a seat belt when you drive?*
> B: **Yes, you should.**

> people / cross the street when the light is red
> A: **Should** *people* **cross** *the street when the light is red?*
> B: **No, they shouldn't.**

1. people / drive slowly when it rains
2. you / drive fast on a crowded street
3. you / look at your passengers when you drive
4. drivers / pay attention to traffic signs when they drive

5. you / swim after you eat
6. you / cover your mouth when you sneeze
7. you / stand under a tree during a storm
8. children / disagree with their parents

Why doesn't Susan want these cars? Look at the example and then complete the conversations.

Salesman: What about this car?
Susan: I don't think so. **It's too impractical.**

1. Salesman: Here's a nice car.
   Susan: No. _____.

2. Salesman: What about this one?
   Susan: Uh uh. _____.

3. Salesman: This is a very nice car.
   Susan: It's nice, but _____.

4. Salesman: I'm sure you'll like this car.
   Susan: I don't think so. _____.

5. Salesman: Why don't you look at this one?
   Susan: Sorry. _____.

6. Salesman: Do you like this car?
   Susan: No. _____.

LESSON
2
Stop the car!

Look at the pictures. Then listen as you read the conversation.

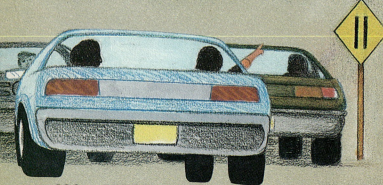

Susan: Well, it wasn't easy, but I finally bought a car.

Lucy: Congratulations! Which one is it?

Susan: It's right over there, next to the wall.

Lucy: Is that big black car yours?

Susan: No. That belongs to Oscar. Do you see the little blue one? That's mine. Come on. Let's go for a ride.

Lucy: Susan! Stop the car!

Susan: Why should I stop?

Lucy: Because you just passed a STOP sign.

Susan: Oh, no. I didn't see it.

Lucy: Well, you really should be careful. A STOP sign means you must stop the car.

Susan: Yes, I know. I'm sorry.

Lucy: Susan! The NO PASSING sign! You mustn't pass other cars here.

Susan: Oh, right. OK. I'll be careful. I promise.

Complete each sentence with the correct pronoun. Look at the examples.

> It belongs to me. It's **mine.**
> It belongs to him. It's **his.**
> It belongs to her. It's **hers.**
> It belongs to us. It's **ours.**
> It belongs to you. It's **yours.**
> It belongs to them. It's **theirs.**

1. Hey! That's my sweater! It belongs to me! It's _____!

2. I'm sorry, you can't use this radio. It belongs to my husband. It's _____.

3. Don't take those clothes. They belong to us. They're _____.

4. Please give me those books. They belong to me. They're _____!

5. Excuse me, but this isn't my hat. It belongs to that man. It's _____.

6. These tennis balls belong to Lynn and Keiko. They're _____.

7. This dog doesn't belong to me. It belongs to that woman. It's _____.

8. Our new baby! He's really cute, and he belongs to us! He's really _____.

Point out things in the classroom and practice this conversation. ▣

> **A: Whose** *sweater* **is** *this (that)?*
> **B: It's** *Gina's (hers).*
>
> **A: Whose** *books* **are** *these (those)?*
> **B: They're** *mine.*

Choose the correct word in the parentheses.

MY FIRST CAR

I wanted a car very badly. (**1.** Me, My, Mine) parents and (**2.** me, my, mine) brother John had trucks. John's truck was great. (**3.** Him, His) was red with big tires. He drove to school every day with (**4.** him, his) girlfriend. Mom and Dad's truck was ten years old. They used (**5.** them, their, theirs) on the farm and for short trips to the store. (**6.** Them, Their, Theirs) truck wasn't much fun, but it worked.

(**7.** Me, My, Mine) sister had (**8.** her, hers) own car, too. (**9.** Her, Hers) was a small, old Japanese car, but it was economical. My grandfather gave (**10.** it, its) to (**11.** her, hers) because he was too old to drive.

I can remember (**12.** me, my, mine) first car very well. There was an ad in the newspaper, and I called the owner. It was an old jeep. It was in a garage, and it was very dirty. (**13.** It, Its) tires were flat, and it needed paint. But it was love at first sight.

I fixed the jeep's tires and painted (**14.** it, its) yellow. I was really excited because it belonged to (**15.** me, my, mine). I spent (**16.** me, my, mine) happiest days in that jeep. There were a lot of great cars in the school parking lot, but they weren't as nice as (**17.** me, my, mine).

Listen to the questions about the article in exercise 3. Choose the correct answers. 🔲

1. a. Two—one brother and one sister.
   b. One brother.
   c. He didn't have any.

2. a. Yes, he was.
   b. No, he wasn't.
   c. It didn't say.

3. a. Probably in the city.
   b. Probably in the country.
   c. It didn't say.

4. a. A new Japanese car.
   b. An old Japanese car.
   c. A big, economical car.

5. a. John's.
   b. The author's.
   c. The author's sister's.

6. a. For two years.
   b. In high school.
   c. It didn't say.

What do these traffic signs mean? Complete the sentences with *must* or *mustn't*. Look at the examples.

You **must** stop.

You **mustn't** pass.

1. You _____ turn right here.

2. You _____ drive a truck here.

3. You _____ drive 55 miles per hour or slower.

4. You _____ park here.

5. You _____ enter here.

6. You _____ make a left turn here.

Complete these sentences with *can, can't, should, shouldn't, must,* or *mustn't*.

THESE THINGS ARE POSSIBLE:

1. You _____ drive a car if you have a license.
2. You _____ swim in the ocean.
3. I _____ use a computer, but I want to learn.

IT'S A GOOD IDEA TO DO THESE THINGS, BUT IT'S YOUR CHOICE:

4. You _____ drive safely.
5. You _____ swim after you eat a big meal.
6. I _____ learn about computers. They are the machines of the future.

YOU DON'T HAVE A CHOICE, SO YOU HAVE TO DO THESE THINGS:

7. You _____ take a test to get a driver's license.
8. You _____ swim if there are sharks in the water.
9. I _____ use a computer. I'm a computer programmer.

Do you agree or disagree?

Do you know the answers to the questions on the driver's license exam?

STATE DEPARTMENT OF MOTOR VEHICLES
DRIVER'S LICENSE
WRITTEN EXAMINATION

DIRECTIONS: Print and sign your name. There are eight questions on this examination. Circle the letter of your answer. There is only one correct answer for each question. *Read carefully*.

Print Your Name   Sign Your Name   Date

_____   _____   _____

1. A good driver always
   a. drives slower than the speed limit.
   b. lets other cars go first.
   c. pays attention to the other drivers on the road.

2. Why is it dangerous to drive at night?
   a. There is more traffic.
   b. You can't see well.
   c. People drive faster.

3. If you feel tired, you should
   a. drive faster and get there quickly.
   b. follow the car in front of you.
   c. open the window or stop and take a rest.

4. If the minimum speed limit is 40 miles per hour, you shouldn't
   a. go 40 mph.
   b. go 30 mph.
   c. go 50 mph.

5. What should you do if you have an accident?
   a. Help the people in the other car.
   b. Get the other person's name and address.
   c. Both a and b.

6. Which of these is dangerous to drink if you're driving?
   a. Alcohol.
   b. Tea and coffee.
   c. Both a and b.

7. What should you do if you have to drive in a bad rain storm?
   a. Close the windows so the rain doesn't come in.
   b. Wear a raincoat.
   c. Turn on your lights and drive slowly.

8. When a car wants to pass you, you should
   a. drive slower.
   b. drive faster.
   c. continue at the same speed.

Decide how you feel about the statements below. Then discuss your answers.

DO YOU AGREE OR DISAGREE?	AGREE	STRONGLY AGREE	DISAGREE	STRONGLY DISAGREE
1. Men are better drivers than women.				
2. Many big cities are crowded, dirty, and noisy. People shouldn't have cars in these cities.				
3. Teenagers aren't safe drivers.				
4. Seat belts save lives. You should get a ticket if you drive without a seat belt.				
5. People over 70 years old shouldn't have driver's licenses.				

EXERCISE 3

Pretend you and your partner write an advice column for a newspaper. The advice column is called "Dear Madeline." Read the letters. Then answer them.

DEAR MADELINE *By Madeline MacRae*

1

Dear Madeline,

My friend is teaching me to drive. I studied the driver's manual, but I make a lot of mistakes when I drive. I'm worried about my friend's car, and I'm afraid she's angry at me. What should I do?

HELP

2

Dear Madeline,

My mother is 70 years old. She lives alone, but she isn't well. If she moves into our house, my daughters (8 and 16 years old) will have to sleep in the same room. My wife and my mother fight a lot. What should I do?

CONFUSED SON

3

Dear Madeline,

My daughter, Jane, is 4 years old. She goes to school from 9-12 every morning. I'm bored at home, but if I go back to work, we'll need a babysitter for Jane in the afternoon. My husband thinks I should stay home. What should I do?

BORED AT HOME

Dear Help,

Dear Confused Son,

Dear Bored at Home,

"Help Line" is a special radio program. People call "Help Line" for advice about their problems. Listen to the program and then choose the appropriate person—a, b, or c. 🔲

1. This person called the radio program.
2. This person is rude.
3. This person is probably having problems at work or school.
4. This person is patient.
5. This person makes a lot of excuses.
6. This person thinks Becky should talk to her boyfriend.
7. Maybe this person has another girlfriend.
8. This person thinks communication is the best answer to the problem.

a. Becky
b. The radio program host
c. Jim

EXERCISE 5

Read the letter. One sentence in each paragraph doesn't fit because the information isn't necessary. Which sentence is it?

Dear Barbara,

It was nice to talk to you the other day. I'm glad everything is going well, and I'm glad that you're happy in Dallas. Houston is nice, too.

I know you like to visit interesting places so you must come to Miami. It's a friendly town with a lot of things to do. There are good restaurants, wonderful beaches, a terrific sea aquarium, and an excellent zoo. Do you like to swim? And the night life is great for single people.

You should plan to stay with us. We would like to have you, and you can stay as long as you want. You should come in the spring or the fall because the weather is best then. It is cold in other parts of the United States during those seasons.

There is a good airport in Miami. I'll send you some tourist information about Miami. I think you'll love it so let me know if you can come and visit.

Love,
Ellen

Now write a letter to a friend in another city.

1. Tell a friend he or she must come to your city. Say why.

2. Tell your friend he or she should plan to stay with you.
3. Tell your friend the best time of year to visit.

4. Tell your friend you'll send pictures or tourist information.
5. Don't give unnecessary information.

SHOULD

Affirmative and Negative Statements

I You He She We They	should shouldn't (should not)	get	a car.

Information (Wh-) Questions

What Which car	should	I	buy?

Yes/No Questions

Should	you	wear	a seat belt when you drive?
	people	cross	the street when the light is red?

Short Answers

Yes, you **should**.
No, they **shouldn't**.

MUST

I You He She We They	must mustn't (must not)	stop	here.

CONTRAST: *CAN, SHOULD,* AND *MUST*

You **can drive** a car if you have a license.
You **should drive** safely.
You **must take** a test to get a driver's license.

WHOSE

Whose	sweater is this?	It's Gina's.
	books are these?	They're hers.

POSSESSIVE PRONOUNS

It belongs to me. It's **mine**.
It belongs to him. It's **his**.
It belongs to her. It's **hers**.
It belongs to us. It's **ours**.
It belongs to you. It's **yours**.
It belongs to them. It's **theirs**.

TOO

It's **too** impractical.
It's **too** hard to drive.
You shouldn't decide **too** quickly.

Vocabulary

accident
advice
air conditioning
airline
alcohol
another
article
author
choice
communication
confused
crowded
driver's license
entry
everyone (everybody)
examination (exam)
exhausted
farm
finally
forever
gas station
host
impractical
jeep
manual
maybe
minimum
motor vehicle
night life
ocean
over (more than)
owner
parking lot
passenger
people
person
practical
radio program (host)
raincoat
sea aquarium
seat belt

shark
speed limit
sports car
storm
strongly
teenager
tourist information
town
traffic sign
ugly
unnecessary
without
worried
written
zoo

Come on.
congratulations (on)
I can/can't afford . . .
It was love at first sight.
Let's go for a ride.
Let's go get a cup of coffee.
Make up your mind.
mph (miles per hour)
So what?

VERBS

belong
continue
cover
disagree
enter
fight [fought]
follow
park
pass
plan (to)
save
sneeze
spend [spent]
turn on

TALKING ABOUT ADVISABILITY

She should buy an economical car.
She shouldn't buy an expensive foreign car.
She likes to drive fast so she should buy a sports car.

TALKING ABOUT POSSESSIONS

Whose sweater is this?
   It's Gina's.
   It's mine.

ASKING FOR AND GIVING ADVICE

Should you wear a seat belt when you drive?
   Yes, you should.

REJECTING A SUGGESTION

What about this car?
   I don't think so. It's too impractical.

TALKING ABOUT OBLIGATION OR NECESSITY

You must stop at a stop sign.
You mustn't pass at a no passing sign.

LESSON
1

Why did you have to get up so early?

Look at the picture. Then listen as you read the conversation.

Lucy: My kids drive me crazy! They complain all the time. They want their own television. They want a computer. They want this. They want that.

Pierre: Why not? A lot of people have those things.

Lucy: Well, when I was their age, I didn't. We couldn't afford them. We lived on a farm and I worked hard. I had to get up at 5 o'clock.

Pierre: Five o'clock? Why did you have to get up so early?

Lucy: Well, it was a small farm and everybody had to help. I fed the chickens, and sometimes I had to milk the cows. Then I had to get ready for school.

Pierre: I guess I had it easy. I could sleep late, and I didn't have to do any work around the house.

Choose the correct word or words in each sentence.

1. When Lucy was young, she probably (had/didn't have) a television.
2. When Pierre was young, he probably (had/didn't have) a television.
3. Lucy's family probably (had/didn't have) a lot of money.
4. Pierre's family probably (had/didn't have) a lot of money.

5. When Lucy was young, she (had to/didn't have to) get up early.
6. When Pierre was young, he (had to/didn't have to) get up early.
7. When Lucy was young, she (had to/didn't have to) work around the farm.
8. When Pierre was young, he (had to/didn't have to) work around the house.

Complete the sentences with *had to* or *didn't have to* and the verbs in parentheses. 📼

When Lucy was a little girl, she **had to milk** the cows.

When Pierre was a little boy, he **didn't have to work** around the house.

1. When Lucy was a little girl, she (feed) the chickens.

2. When Pierre was a little boy, he (get up) early.

3. When Keiko was young, she (make) her own breakfast.

4. Roberto (deliver) papers after school when he was young.

5. Tetsuo and his sister (practice) every day.

6. Gina (do) any homework when she was little.

7. When she was little, Olga (work) in her father's store.

What about you?
When I was young/ little, I _____.

Listen and complete this conversation. ▭

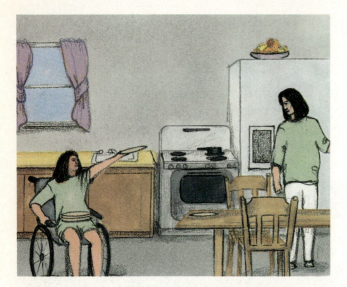

Isabel: Mom, do I really have to help Dad?
Olga: Yes, you do. ¹_____, and he needs your help.
Isabel: Did you have to help your parents when you were my age?
Olga: Yes. As a matter of fact, ²_____.
Isabel: When did you have to work?
Olga: ³_____.
Isabel: What did you have to do?
Olga: I cleaned around the store, and ⁴_____.
Isabel: What else did you have to do?
Olga: ⁵_____.
Isabel: Why did you have to do that?
Olga: ⁶_____, and she couldn't do it.

Practice this conversation.

A: **Did you have to help** your parents when you were younger?
B: _____.

A: **What did you have to do?**
B: _____.
A: **When/why/what else . . .?**
B: _____.

Complete each conversation with a sentence from the list below. Then practice the conversations. ▭

a. Why was it so expensive?
b. Why did you have to get up so early?
c. It was so good!
d. Why did you have to work so much?
e. It's so big!
f. How did you do it so quickly?
g. I can't believe you ate so many.

A: I had to get up at 5 o'clock when I was little.
B: Five o'clock? Why did you have to get up so early?
A: I had to feed the animals.

1. A: I love this sweater. _____
   B: But it's too big, isn't it?
   A: No. I like big clothes.

2. A: I really liked the movie. _____
   B: But it was too long, wasn't it?
   A: Oh no, I like long movies.

(continued)

3. A: I had to work after school every day when I was little.
   B: Every day? _____
   A: Because my family didn't have a lot of money.

4. A: I ate three pieces of cake.
   B: Three pieces? _____
   A: Yeah. I hope I don't get sick.

5. A: I paid $600 for my new TV.
   B: $600? _____
   A: Because it's so big.

6. A: I finished my test in ten minutes.
   B: Ten minutes? _____
   A: It was easy, and I knew all the answers.

What do you think? Complete the sentences with *could*, *couldn't*, *can*, or *can't*.

When Roberto was a little boy, he **couldn't** type well. Today he is a reporter, and he **can** type very well.

1. Pierre _____ sleep late when he was younger, but now he _____ sleep late because he has to work.
2. When Keiko was in elementary school, she _____ speak English. Now she is studying in the United States, and she _____ speak English very well.
3. When Marco was a little boy, he _____ play soccer very well. Today he _____ play very well.
4. When Lynn was younger she _____ afford to buy a camera, but she has a good job now, and she _____ afford several cameras.
5. Tetsuo _____ play the piano very well when he was little. Then he began to practice every day, and now he _____ play very well.
6. When Mrs. Brennan was in college, she _____ sing very well. Today she _____ sing well because she doesn't practice.

Find out about your classmates. Use this conversation and your own ideas.

A: **When you were younger, could you** *speak English*?
B: **Yes, I could./No, I couldn't.** OR
   No, I couldn't, but I can now. OR
   No, I couldn't, and I still can't.

A surprise party

Listen as you read the conversation and the note. 📼

Keiko: Lynn, did you know that Tetsuo is going back to Japan?
Lynn: No. When?
Keiko: At the end of this English course. I just saw Roberto and Tony.
They're having a surprise party for him. Listen to this.

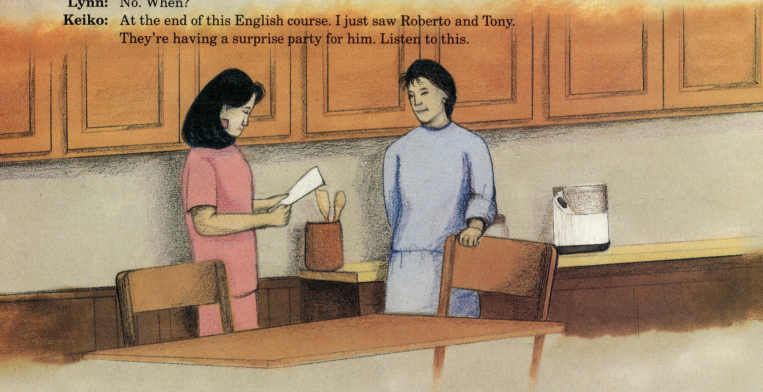

Dear Classmates,
   Tetsuo has a great job offer, and he is going
back to Japan at the end of this course. We are
going to have a surprise party for him, and we'd
like to invite all of his classmates and Mr. and
Mrs. Brennan.
   The party will be at our place next Friday
night at 7:00. If anyone would like to help,
please let us know. We've got enough glasses, but
we need a few plates. And has anybody got a
portable stereo? Ours is broken.
                    Roberto and Tony

Complete the questions and give the answers as in the examples. Then listen to each exchange. 📼

> **A:** Tetsuo **is** going back to Japan, **isn't he?**
> **B:** **Yes, he is.**
> **A:** He **isn't** going to take the next English course, **is he?**
> **B:** **No, he isn't.**
> **A:** The party **will** be a surprise, **won't it?**
> **B:** **Yes, it will.**
> **A:** The party **won't** be at Tetsuo's place, **will it?**
> **B:** **No, it won't.**

1. A: Tetsuo is going to teach music in Japan, _____?

   B: _____.
2. A: He isn't going to teach in Dallas, _____?

   B: _____.

3. A: Roberto and Tony will miss him, _____?
   B: _____.
4. A: In fact, all of his classmates are going to miss him, _____?
   B: _____.
5. A: Tetsuo won't forget Dallas, _____?
   B: _____.

Now ask your partner these questions.

6. We'll finish this book soon, _____?
7. The next course will begin on (date), _____?
8. You're going to take the next course, _____?

Tony and Roberto checked the things they've got for the surprise party. Look at their list and make sentences with *have ('ve) got* and *haven't got*.

✓ 17 glasses
a stereo
✓ 9 plates
napkins
✓ a camera

> Tony and Roberto **have got** 17 (some) glasses.
> They **haven't got** a stereo.

1. Tony and Roberto _____.
2. They _____.
3. They _____.

Keiko is going to help Tony and Roberto with the surprise party. Look at her list and make sentences with *has('s) got* and *hasn't got*.

✓ 17 spoons
records
✓ 4 plates
camera
✓ stereo

> Keiko's **got** some spoons.
> She **hasn't got** any records.

4. Keiko _____.
5. She _____.
6. She _____.

There are seventeen people at the party. Do Tony and Roberto have enough of everything? Look at the picture and the examples and make sentences.

They've got **enough** glasses.
They haven't got **enough** plates. They need four **more**.

Tony is calling his neighbor, Jeff. Listen and choose the correct answers. 📼

1. Jeff has got
   a. four plates.
   b. eight plates.
   c. no plates.

2. Jeff has got
   a. four cups and saucers.
   b. eight cups and saucers.
   c. no cups and saucers.

3. Jeff has got
   a. eleven knives.
   b. twelve knives.
   c. no knives.

4. Jeff has got
   a. ten forks.
   b. thirteen forks.
   c. no forks.

5. Jeff has got
   a. a lot of paper napkins.
   b. sixteen paper napkins.
   c. no napkins.

6. Jeff has got
   a. sixteen glasses.
   b. eight glasses.
   c. It didn't say.

Olga is in Tony and Roberto's kitchen. She's making punch for the party. Look at the picture and ask and answer Olga's questions. 🔲

Olga: **Have you got any** *oranges*?	**Olga:** **Have you got any** *ice cream*?
Tony: **Yes, we've got** *a lot.*	**Tony:** **Yes, we've got** *a lot.*
Olga: **Have you got any** *lemons*?	**Olga:** **Have you got any** *pineapple juice*?
Tony: **Yes, we've got** *a few.*	**Tony:** **Yes, we've got** *a little.*

a few cherries

a little ginger ale

a little pineapple juice

a few limes

a lot of apple juice

a lot of oranges

a lot of ice

a little sugar

a lot of ice cream

a few lemons

Interview your classmates. Use this conversation as a model. 🔲

A: Have you got a lot of *money in your wallet today*?
B: Yes, I have. OR
No, I haven't. I've only got *a little.* OR
I haven't got any.

Find someone who . . .	Name of Classmate
1. has got a lot of money in his/her wallet today.	_____
2. has got only a little money today.	_____
3. hasn't got any money today.	_____
4. has got a lot of homework to do for tomorrow.	_____
5. hasn't got much homework to do for tomorrow.	_____
6. has got a lot of brothers and sisters.	_____
7. hasn't got any brothers and sisters.	_____
8. has got only one brother or sister.	_____

Goodbye and good luck!

Make a list of things you *could* and *couldn't* do when you were younger.
Then make another list of things you *had to* do.

COULD   COULDN'T
swim   speak English

HAD TO
take out the garbage at home

Now compare your list with your partner's.
Use this conversation as a model.

A: I could *swim.* **Could you?**
B: Yes, I could. /No, I couldn't.

A: I had to *take out the garbage.* **Did you?**
B: Yes, I did. /No, I didn't.

Listen to this conversation and
write the woman's questions.

When you finish, ask your
partner the questions. Your
partner will answer with his or
her own information.

Woman: 1_____?
   Man: Yes, I think so.
Woman: 2_____?
   Man: I'm going to Miami. I'm leaving on Saturday.
Woman: 3_____?
   Man: I'm going to visit friends. We'll probably just go to the beach and relax.
Woman: That sounds good. 4_____?
   Man: In a week.
Woman: 5_____?
   Man: Sure.
   Lucy: 6_____?
   Man: Of course not.

EXERCISE 3

Work with a group. Plan a party for the last day of class.

1. First choose a day and time for the party.
   A: When should we have the party?
   B: _____.

2. Next make a list of things you need for the party.
   A: What do we need?
   B: _____.

3. Then find out who can bring each thing.
   A: Who's got a *stereo*?
   B: I've got *one*.

   A: Who's got *some cassettes*?
   C: I've got a *few/some*.

   A: OK. Who can bring *some soda*?
   D: I can bring a *little/some*.

EXERCISE 4

Read this article from a student newspaper. Then correct these mistakes:

1. The first paragraph needs two commas and four periods.
2. The second paragraph has an unnecessary sentence.
3. The third paragraph needs eight capital letters.

UNIVERSITY PRESS

GOODBYE AND GOOD LUCK

Jun Ogawa of Kyoto Japan will return to his country on June 18 Mr Ogawa is a student at the University English Center He will finish his present course on Friday Mr. Owaga is a well-known architect and he has designed buildings in Japan and in many countries around the world. He likes the United States very much. When he isn't working, he likes to work in his garden or watch baseball games.

mr. ogawa is married and he has two daughters: sumi, 9, and yoko, 7. his wife, michiko, works for japan airlines.

EXERCISE 5

Write an article about a classmate. Use the article in exercise 4 as a model and answer these questions:

Paragraph 1: Where is your classmate from, and what will your classmate do after this English course ends?

Paragraph 2: What does your classmate do for a living (or what kind of student is your classmate)? What does your classmate do during his or her free time?

Paragraph 3: Give information about your classmate's spouse (or girlfriend or boyfriend) and children.

EXERCISE 6

Answer the questions about yourself, your class, and your book.

1. What was the funniest thing that happened during this class?
2. What was your favorite unit or lesson?
3. Which unit or lesson did you hate?
4. What was the most important thing you learned?
5. What was the most important thing that happened to you outside of school?
6. Which do you like best: speaking, reading, or writing English?
7. What do you like to do the best in class: work alone, work with a partner, or work in a group?
8. Finish this sentence: English is _____.

HAD TO

Affirmative and Negative Statements

I You He She We They	had to didn't have to	feed	the animals.

Yes/No Questions

Did	you	have to	help	your parents?

Short Answers

Yes, I **did**./No, I **didn't**.

Information (Wh-) Questions

When	did	you	have to	work?

COULD (PAST ABILITY)

Affirmative and Negative Statements

I You He She We They	could couldn't (could not)	swim.

Yes/No Questions

(When you were younger,)	could	you	speak	English?
I could ski.	Could	you?		

Short Answers

Yes, I **could**. / No, I **couldn't**.

TAG QUESTIONS: FUTURE TENSES (*BE GOING TO* AND *WILL*)

Tetsuo is going back to Japan,	**isn't he?**	Yes, he is.
He isn't going to take the next English course,	**is he?**	No, he isn't.
The party will be a surprise,	**won't it?**	Yes, it will.
The party won't be at Tetsuo's place,	**will it?**	No, it won't.

HAVE GOT

Affirmative and Negative Statements

I You We They	've (have) haven't	got	a stereo.
He She	's (has) hasn't		

Yes/No Questions

Have	you	got	a lot of money?

Short Answers

Yes, I **have**./No, I **haven't**.

Who as Subject
Who's got a stereo?

ENOUGH

They've got **enough** glasses.
They haven't got **enough** plates. They need four more.

A LOT (OF), A LITTLE, AND A FEW

We've got	a lot of	oranges.
	a little	pineapple juice.
	a few	lemons.

SO

Why did you have to get up **so** early?
Why did you have to work **so** much?
The movie was **so** good.

VOCABULARY

animal
anyone
audience
boyfriend
broken
cassette
cow
customer
enough
fork
free time
garden
ginger ale
ice
job offer
lemon
lime
napkin
package
paragraph
pineapple
postcard
reading
record
saucer
speaking
spouse
surprise
unnecessary
well-known
writing

all the time
As a matter of fact,
Good luck.
I had it easy.
My kids drive me crazy!
Of course not.
That sounds good.

VERBS

be [was/were] back
believe
bring [brought]
deliver
get [got] sick
milk

COMMUNICATION SUMMARY

TALKING ABOUT PAST OBLIGATION AND NECESSITY

When I was a little girl, I had to clean my bedroom.
When I was a young, I didn't have to work around the house.
Did you have to help your parents?
    Yes, I did.
What did you have to do?
    I had to take care of my brothers and sisters.

TALKING ABOUT PAST AND PRESENT ABILITY

When Roberto was a little boy, he couldn't type.
Today he is a reporter, and he can type very well.

When you were little, could you speak English?
    Yes, I could.
    No, I couldn't, but I can now.
    No, I couldn't, and I still can't.

EXPRESSING SURPRISE AND INTEREST

Why did you have to get up so early?
    I had to feed the animals.
I love this sweater. It's so big!

ASKING FOR CONFIRMATION

The surprise party won't be at Tetsuo's place, will it?
    No, it won't.
We'll finish this book soon, won't we?
    Yes, we will.
You're going to take the next course, aren't you?
    Yes, I am.

TALKING ABOUT AVAILABILITY

They haven't got a stereo.
Keiko hasn't got any records.
They haven't got enough plates.

TALKING ABOUT QUANTITY

Have you got any oranges?
    Yes, we've got a lot/a few.
Have you got any pineapple juice?
    Yes, we've got a little.

IRREGULAR VERBS

Base Form	Simple Past	Base Form	Simple Past
be	was, were	leave	left
become	became	lend	lent
begin	began	lose	lost
bite	bit	make	made
break	broke	meet	met
bring	brought	pay	paid
build	built	put	put
buy	bought	read	read
catch	caught	ride	rode
choose	chose	ring	rang
come	came	run	ran
cost	cost	say	said
cut	cut	see	saw
do	did	sell	sold
draw	drew	send	sent
drink	drank	shut	shut
drive	drove	sing	sang
eat	ate	sit	sat
fall	fell	sleep	slept
feed	fed	speak	spoke
feel	felt	spend	spent
fight	fought	stand	stood
fly	flew	steal	stole
forget	forgot	swim	swam
get	got	take	took
give	gave	teach	taught
go	went	tell	told
grow	grew	think	thought
have	had	throw	threw
hear	heard	understand	understood
hit	hit	wake up	woke up
hold	held	wear	wore
hurt	hurt	win	won
keep	kept	write	wrote
know	knew		

TAPESCRIPTS
for Listening Comprehension Exercises

UNIT 1

Lesson 1, exercise 7, p. 5

Listen to the interviews. Then complete the chart with the right nationality and occupation.

Roberto: My name is Roberto Rivera. I'm from Puerto Rico, and I'm a reporter. Today we are having a wonderful party, and I'm interviewing my classmates for our school newspaper. First, let's meet Lucy Mendoza. Lucy is from Mexico. She's a nurse. Good evening, Lucy. Are you enjoying the party?

Lucy: Oh, yes. I think that this is an excellent party. Everybody is having a good time.

Roberto: And this is Keiko Abe. Keiko is a secretary. She's from Japan. What do you think about the party, Keiko?

Keiko: I think it's great. The food is great. The music is great. The people are great.

Roberto: Here's Keiko's roommate, Lynn Wang. Lynn is a photographer from China. Are you enjoying the party, Lynn?

Lynn: Yes, I am. And I know that everybody else is enjoying it, too. Everybody is dancing and enjoying the food.

Roberto: This is Carlos Perez. Carlos is from Colombia. He's a carpenter. Carlos, I understand that you don't like the party.

Carlos: Oh, I like the party. I think everybody is having fun. I'm just sad. I hear these songs from my country and I feel lonely.

Roberto: Here's Pravit Soongwang. Pravit is Thai. He's a mechanic. What about you, Pravit? How do you feel about this party?

Pravit: I feel that all parties are a lot of work. In fact, I don't really like parties.

Now listen again and match the opinions below with the right person in the chart.

Lesson 2, exercise 3, p. 7

Ann Brennan helped the students with the party yesterday. What about her husband? Listen and complete the sentences with the verbs in the list.

Jerry Brennan *worked* hard yesterday morning.

1. First he fixed the car in the garage.
2. Then he painted some bookcases in the basement.
3. Then he cleaned the attic.
4. Next he washed the clothes in the laundry room.
5. Then he called his mother.
6. Next he prepared lunch in the kitchen.
7. Finally, of course, he rested in the bedroom.

Lesson 3, exercise 3, p. 10

Listen to the conversation. Then complete the invitation.

Woman: Hi. I'm sorry I'm late.

Man: It doesn't matter. Don't worry about it. Would you like something to drink?

Woman: No, thank you. You know, Richard's birthday is next week.

Man: Really? Let's have a party. He's really unhappy right now. He misses his friends and family.

Woman: Yeah, I know. Well, his birthday is May fifth. That's next Thursday. Let's have the party then.

Man: I can't. I'm busy that night. What about Friday, the sixth?

Woman: Friday's good. What time? About seven o'clock?

Man: Yeah. Seven is fine. And let's invite everybody in the class.

Woman: OK. Where do you want to have the party? At your house?

Man: Yeah. Do you know the address?

Woman: No. What is it?

Man: 210 West Street. And my phone number is 555-8675.

Woman: Great!

Lesson 1, exercise 5, p. 18

A woman is talking to her family. Listen to the conversation. Which things did the woman's family do? Answer Yes or No.

Woman: Did you finish your jobs around the house?

Man: Uh, I think so.

Boy: Yeah.

Woman: Did anyone fix the car?

Man: I fixed the car.

Woman: Did anyone fix the refrigerator?

Boy: No, I didn't have time.

Woman: Did anyone clean the bathroom?

Girl: I did. But I didn't clean the kitchen.

Woman: Well, you can clean it later. Did anyone pick up the mess in the living room?

Boy: Uh. No. But I picked up the mess in the dining room.

Woman: Did anyone call Grandma?

Girl: I called her. She says hello to everyone.

Woman: Did you talk to Grandpa?

Girl: No. He didn't want to talk. He isn't feeling well today.

Woman: Did you shop for lunch?

Man: Yes. But I didn't buy anything for dinner.

Woman: We don't have anything in the house for dinner, do we?

Man: No.

Woman: Well, I guess you're going to the store again after lunch, aren't you?

Man: Yes, dear.

Woman: And don't forget to clean the living room!

Boy: Yes, Mom.

Woman: And the kitchen!

Girl: Yes, Mom.

Lesson 2, exercise 4, p. 20

Listen and complete this conversation.

Lucy: You didn't come to class yesterday, Pravit. What happened?

Pravit: I had a bad day yesterday so I stayed home. To begin with, I didn't hear my alarm so I woke up late.

Lucy: Oh.

Pravit: I got up and got dressed quickly, but I put on one blue sock and one white sock so I had to change my socks.

Lucy: Gee.

Pravit: That's not all. I fell in the kitchen and hit my head so I had to go to the doctor. And I didn't have time to eat my breakfast.

Lucy: That's too bad.

Pravit: Yeah. And I forgot my wallet so I had to go back home again. And on my way home, a police officer gave me a ticket.

Lucy: Wow! What did you do?

Pravit: When I got home, I took off my clothes, put on my pajamas, and went back to bed!

Lesson 3, exercise 2, p. 22

Listen to all of Mary's and Bob's conversation from exercise 1. Choose the correct dates in the chart.

Mary: Hi, Bob. How are you?

Bob: Fine, thanks.

Mary: It's a beautiful day, isn't it?

Bob: Yes, it is.

Mary: You aren't busy, are you?

Bob: No, I'm not. I'm just reading my English notes.

Mary: Do you have a test tomorrow?

Bob: No, I don't, but this lesson is very interesting.

Mary: What's very interesting?

Bob: Well, did you know that Columbus discovered America in 1492?

Mary: Of course.

Bob: OK. When did the United States declare its independence from England?

Mary: In 1676?

Bob: No. In 1776.

Mary: Oh.

Bob: When did Alexander Graham Bell make the first telephone call?

Mary: Let's see. He made the first call in 1876.

Bob: Uh-huh. And when did Thomas Edison invent the electric light bulb?

Mary: Gee. I don't know.

Bob: In 1879. What about this? When did man first walk on the moon?

Mary: Oh, I know that. That's an important date for everybody. 1969.

Bob: Do you remember their names?

Mary: Neil Armstrong and Edwin Aldrin.

Lesson 1, exercise 5, p. 28

Listen to the conversation and fill in the missing words.

Keiko: Show me the pictures of the party.
Lynn: Pierre has the pictures.
Keiko: No, He doesn't. I saw him last night.
Lynn: Oh, then you met her.
Keiko: Who?
Lynn: Pierre's girlfriend.
Keiko: No. She wasn't with him. What about the pictures?
Lynn: Well, then I don't remember what I did with it.
Keiko: With what?
Lynn: My camera bag. I had my camera bag when I saw them.
Keiko: Saw who?
Lynn: Oscar and Tony. I showed them the pictures. Then I put them in my camera bag. By the way, Oscar and Tony invited us to a picnic.
Keiko: Invited who? The class?
Lynn: No. You and me. Oscar thinks you're cute.
Keiko: What? Oscar and Tony both have girlfriends!
Lynn: I know, so I told them no.

Lesson 2, exercise 3, p. 32

Listen and choose the correct answer.

1. **Man:** That brown dog is cute. Let's take it home.
   Woman: I don't think that's a good idea. He's very big, and our apartment is very small.
   Man: You're right. He is very big so let's take the small one.

2. **Friend:** Those gold earrings are beautiful.
   Lucy: I know, but I don't have much money.
   Friend: What about these silver ones?
   Lucy: Yes. I like them very much.

3. **Tetsuo:** I like the shirts with short sleeves, and I like the ones with long sleeves, too.
   Friend: But you're going to Hawaii, aren't you?

Tetsuo: Yes.
Friend: Well, you don't need long-sleeved shirts in Hawaii.
Tetsuo: You're right.

4. **Hector:** The car with two doors is nice. And I like the color.
   Olga: Don't forget we have three kids.
   Hector: That's true. I guess we need the one with four doors.
   Olga: And it's a nice color, too.

5. **Student 1:** Let's all go to the movies. There's a good one at the Regency.
   Student 2: But it's in Spanish, and Lynn and Keiko don't speak Spanish.
   Student 1: Oh, right. Well, what's playing at Cinema One?
   Student 2: A western. I don't remember the name.

6. **Roberto:** Hey, those are great sunglasses.
   Salesman: Yes, they are. And they come in green and gray.
   Roberto: Could I have the green ones, please?
   Salesman: Sure. Here you are.

Lesson 3, exercise 2, p. 34

First try to complete the conversation with the sentences in the list. Then listen and check your answers.

Saleswoman: May I help you?
Man: Yes. I'm looking for a sweater.
Saleswoman: What size?
Man: A medium, I think.
Saleswoman: What color are you looking for?
Man: Green. Dark green.
Saleswoman: Here's a nice one.
Man: Can I try it on?
Saleswoman: Certainly. The dressing room is right over there.

Saleswoman: How does it fit?
Man: It's too tight. Do you have a large?
Saleswoman: Yes. Here you are.
Man: It's fine. I'll take it.
Saleswoman: Cash or charge?
Man: Charge.

Lesson 1, exercise 3, p. 40

Listen to the questions about Spike and Belle. Choose the correct answers.

1. Were Spike and Belle together last night?
2. Was Spike at Butler's Department Store last night?
3. Was Spike alone last night?
4. Was Belle at home last night?
5. Were Belle and Dolores at United Bank?
6. Were they at Butler's?
7. Was there a sale at Butler's?
8. Were the dresses on sale?
9. Was the store open until midnight?
10. Was Spike angry when Belle got home?

Lesson 2, exercise 6, p. 45

Listen and complete the conversation.

Man: Let's take our vacation in the city this year.

Woman: But the weather in the country is nicer than the weather in the city.

Man: All right. Let's take our vacation in the country.

Woman: But life in the city is more exciting than life in the country.

Man: Then let's take our vacation in the city.

Woman: But the country is safer than the city for children.

Man: OK, the country.

Woman: However, the people in the city are more interesting than the people in the country. And the restaurants are better than the restaurants in the country.

Man: All right then. The city.

Woman: But the people in the country are friendlier than the people in the city.

Man: Please make up your mind!

Woman: I can't.

Man: You know, I have an idea. Let's not take a vacation at all! Let's stay home!

Lesson 3, exercise 2, p. 46

Read the article and guess the missing words. Then listen and correct your guesses.

A lot of people think that a house is nicer than an apartment. I don't agree. I prefer an apartment. I lived in an apartment for many years. The rooms were small, but they were very comfortable. And I didn't need much furniture. The building was near the bus stop, so it was easy to get to work. The building was very modern, and my rent wasn't expensive. My neighbors were friendly.

Two years ago, I moved to a house. The house is nice, but I pay a lot of money to the bank every month. The rooms are very big, and I had to buy a lot of furniture. The house is very far from transportation, so it isn't easy to get to work. And I'm lonely. I never see my neighbors.

Lesson 1, exercise 3, p. 52

What's the problem? First listen to the example. Then listen to the conversations and complete the sentences.

Clerk: May I help you?
Gina: Yes, please. I'd like to return these shoes.
Clerk: Certainly. What's the problem with them?
Gina: Your ad says they're the most comfortable shoes in the world, but they aren't comfortable at all.

1. **Clerk:** May I help you?
   Alan: Yes, please. I'd like to return this computer game.
   Clerk: Sure. What's the problem with it?
   Alan: Your ad says it's the easiest computer game in the world, but it isn't easy at all.

2. **Clerk:** May I help you?
   Oscar: Yes, please. I'd like to return these books.
   Clerk: Of course. What's the problem with them?
   Oscar: Your ad says they're the most interesting books in the world, but they aren't interesting at all.

3. **Clerk:** May I help you?
   Roberto: Yes, please. I'd like to return this pillow.
   Clerk: Of course. What's the problem with it?
   Roberto: Your ad says it's the softest pillow in the world, but it isn't soft at all.

4. **Clerk:** May I help you?
   Lucy: Yes, please. I'd like to return these curtains.
   Clerk: Certainly. What's the problem with them?
   Lucy: Your ad says they're the prettiest curtains in the world, but they aren't pretty at all.

Lesson 2, exercise 3, p. 55

What's the matter with Oscar's patients? Listen to the example. Then listen and complete the conversations.

Oscar: What's the matter?
Tetsuo: I hurt my arm.
Oscar: Oh, that's too bad.

1. **Oscar:** What's the matter, Mr. Brennan?
   Jerry: I hurt my back.
   Oscar: Oh, that's too bad.

2. **Oscar:** What's the matter?
   Olga: I hurt my leg.
   Oscar: I'm sorry to hear that.

3. **Oscar:** What's the matter, Tony?
   Tony: I hurt my hand.
   Oscar: Oh, that's too bad.

4. **Oscar:** What's the matter?
   Lynn: I hurt my knee.
   Oscar: Oh, I'm sorry to hear that.

5. **Oscar:** What's the matter, Susan?
   Susan: I hurt my foot.
   Oscar: Oh, that's too bad.

6. **Oscar:** What's the matter?
   Pravit: I hurt my shoulder.
   Oscar: Well, I'm sorry to hear that.

Lesson 3, exercise 2, p. 58

Listen to the conversation and choose the correct answer.

Nurse: Doctor's office. May I help you?
John: Yes. My name is John Carver. I'd like to make an appointment to see Dr. Carter.
Nurse: What seems to be the problem?
John: I don't feel very well. I guess I have a bad cold.
Nurse: Well, Dr. Carter has an opening at 3:00 this afternoon. Can you come in then?
John: At 3:00? No, I'm sorry I can't. How about tomorrow afternoon?
Nurse: Let's see. Tomorrow afternoon at 2:00?
John: Yes, that would be fine.
Nurse: All right. See you then.
John: Oh, excuse me. What's your exact address?
Nurse: 1030 Johnson Street, 2nd floor.
John: Thank you.

Lesson 1, exercise 6, p. 65

Try to guess the missing words. Then listen and check your guesses.

A LOOK AT THE FUTURE

The houses of tomorrow are not going to be the same as they are today. They are going to be very different. They are going to have computers and robots. The robots are going to repair and clean the houses. We are going to connect our appliances and lights to computers. If we leave our homes and forget to turn off our stoves or electric coffee pots, we are going to call our computers on the telephone and turn off the appliances. If we have to work late, we are going to call our homes and turn on the lights.

Lesson 2, exercise 5, p. 68

Listen and write the first eight lines of the conversation.

Man: Where are you going?
Woman: I'm going to Los Angeles.
Man: Do you live there?
Woman: No. I'm going to visit my sister.
Man: Where does your sister live?
Woman: She lives near the beach.
Man: Is your sister going to meet you at the airport?
Woman: No. She's going to be at work so I'm going to take a taxi.
Man: Listen, I'm going to rent a car. Would you like a ride?
Woman: Oh, no thank you.
Man: Are you sure?
Woman: Yes. But thanks anyway.

Lesson 3, exercise 4, p. 71 (answers in parentheses)

Listen to the questions about New York City. Choose the correct answers.

1. Where is Manhattan? (c. Both a and b.)
2. How many people live on the island of Manhattan? (a. 3 million.)
3. How many people work on the island of Manhattan? (b. 4 million.)
4. Who designed the Statue of Liberty? (a. Bartholdi.)
5. Where did the Statue of Liberty come from? (c. Guide didn't say.)
6. Are the World Trade Center buildings the tallest buildings in the world? (b. No.)
7. Is the South Street Seaport a busy port? (b. No.)
8. What can you do at the South Street Seaport? (c. Both a and b.)

Lesson 1, exercise 4, p. 76 (with completions in parentheses)

Listen and choose the letter of the words you hear.

1. a. We can ski (and we can play tennis).
2. b. Tetsuo can't play the guitar (, but he can play the piano very well).
3. b. Gina can't go to the party (because she's sick).
4. a. A lot of students can type (and use computers).
5. b. Lynn can't take our pictures today (, but she can take them tomorrow).
6. b. We can't walk there (because it's very far and it's going to rain).
7. a. He can speak English very well (so he doesn't study very much).
8. b. I can't help you with your homework (because I don't understand it).

Lesson 2, exercise 4, p. 80

Listen and complete the conversation.

Man: Would you like to go to a movie tonight?
Keiko: Oh, I'm sorry. I can't. I've got to study.
Man: Oh, do you go to school?
Keiko: Yes. I'm studying English and Business.
Man: That's interesting. Well, do you want to go to the beach on Saturday?
Keiko: No, I really can't. But thanks anyway.
Man: Well, could I have your telephone number so I can call you sometime?
Keiko: No, I don't think that's a good idea because I'm never home.
Man: I see. Well, nice talking to you.
Keiko: Bye.

Lesson 3, exercise 3, p. 82

Listen to the job interview. Then complete these notes.

Woman: How many years of experience do you have?
Man: About five.
Woman: Ummh. And where did you work before?
Man: Well, I worked at the Grand Cafe for three years, and then I worked at Joe's Place for about two years.
Woman: Why did you leave?
Man: I left my last job because I wanted to work days and they only had jobs at night.
Woman: And why do you want to work here?
Man: One of my friends works here. And she says the people are very nice and the restaurant is very good.
Woman: I see. Do you have any questions you'd like to ask me?
Man: Yes. What's the salary?
Woman: $5.00 an hour plus tips.
Man: What are the hours?
Woman: If you work days, you have to work from 11:00 until 4:30.
Man: And what are the benefits? Is there health insurance?
Woman: Yes. There's health insurance. And you get one sick day a month. You also get two weeks vacation. Do you have any other questions?
Man: No, I think that's all. Thank you.

Lesson 1, exercise 5, p. 88

Listen and complete Lynn's part of the conversation.

Lynn: Well, are you going to marry Frank?
Gina: I don't know.
Lynn: Will you decide soon?
Gina: Yes, I will.
Lynn: Will Frank be a good husband?
Gina: I think that he will. I know he loves me.
Lynn: And will you be happy with Frank?
Gina: Yes. I love him very much.
Lynn: Will your parents be happy?
Gina: No, they won't. That's the problem. They don't like him very much.
Lynn: Well, what are you going to do?
Gina: I don't know.
Lynn: Well, I'm sure Frank wants an answer.
Gina: Yes, he's very patient, but I'll tell him very soon.

Lesson 2, exercise 5, p. 92

First, read the article and try to guess the missing words. Then listen and check your guesses.

FORTUNETELLERS

Many people around the world go to fortunetellers. These people think that fortunetellers will tell them about their futures. There are many kinds of fortunetellers, and they use different ways to tell the future.

The study of palms began several centuries ago in India. Palm readers study the lines and sizes of people's hands to tell the future. Palm readers say that every line has a name and a meaning. A strong head line, for example, means a person is intelligent.

Numerology started in China. It is the study of numbers. Numerologists use people's names and birth dates to explain their personalities and to tell about their pasts and their futures. They give each letter of the alphabet a number from one to nine. Then they add together the numbers in a person's name and birth date to get information about that person.

Graphology is the study of handwriting. Graphologists think the way people write gives information about their personalities. For example, if you write with lines that go up, you'll have a happy life, but if you write with lines that go down, you won't.

Other fortunetellers read cards or tea leaves. Some study the size of clouds and watch the stars and the moon. In any case, fortunetellers have one thing in common: They tell us about the future. However, can they really do this? And, more important, do we really want to know the future?

Lesson 3, exercise 3, p. 95

Tom and his friend Bob are talking about Tom's fiancee Rosa. Listen and choose the best answers.

Bob: So, Tom, are you going to get married or not?
Tom: Yeah, yeah, but Rosa's afraid. She's not sure she wants to get married right now. She can't decide.
Bob: Why not? Is she a Pisces?
Tom: I don't really know much about people's signs.
Bob: So, why can't she decide?
Tom: Well, we're both young, and she likes her job. And, of course, if we have children, she'll have to quit her job.
Bob: Why? A lot of women have kids but don't quit their jobs.
Tom: True, but I don't want Rosa to work.
Bob: Oh. So when will she give you an answer?
Tom: I'm going to her house for dinner Saturday night. She'll tell me then.
Bob: Well, good luck.
Tom: Thanks. What are you going to do this weekend, Bob?
Bob: I'm going fishing with my dad. We'll probably leave early Saturday morning and come back Saturday night.
Tom: What time will you get home?
Bob: Around 7 o'clock. I have a date with my girlfriend at 8:00.
Tom: Will I see you on Sunday?
Bob: Yeah. In fact, why don't we all do something?
Tom: OK. What?
Bob: Oh, I don't know. We can go to a movie or something.
Tom: Fine.

Lesson 1, exercise 2, p. 99

Listen and complete the conversation with *should* or *shouldn't (should not)*.

Salesman: Do you like this sports car?

Susan: Oh, yes. But it's too expensive. I can't afford it.

Salesman: You're young. You should have fun. Are you married?

Susan: No.

Salesman: Then you shouldn't buy a family car right now.

Susan: I know, but I'm very practical. I should buy a car I can use in the future.

Salesman: You're confused, aren't you?

Susan: Yes. So I really shouldn't make a decision right now.

Salesman: I agree. You should think about it.

Susan: Well, I think my friends are tired. We should take a break. Thank you for your help.

Salesman: You're welcome.

Lesson 2, exercise 4, page 104 (with answers in parentheses)

Listen to the questions about the article in exercise 3. Choose the correct answers.

1. How many brothers and sisters did the author have?   (a. Two—one brother and one sister.)
2. Was John married?   (b. No, he wasn't.)
3. Where did the author live?   (b. Probably in the country.)
4. What kind of car did the author's sister have? (b. An old Japanese car.)
5. Whose car was yellow?   (b. The author's.)
6. How long did the author have his jeep? (c. It didn't say.)

Lesson 3, exercise 4, p. 107

"Help Line" is a special radio program. People call "Help Line" for advice about their problems. Listen to the program and then choose the appropriate person—a, b, or c.

Radio: Hello. This is "Help Line." How can I help you?

Caller: Uh . . . Hello. My name's Becky and, well, I'm having a lot of problems with my boyfriend. His name's Jim. Well, he's never on time, and he never pays attention to me when we are together. I mean, he's very rude.

Radio: You're right, Becky, Jim's rude. If he likes you, he should pay attention to you. Is he having a problem at work or at school?

Caller: Well, maybe. I mean, it's possible, but he never says anything. You know, I'm very patient, but I don't think he loves me.

Radio: Why don't you talk to him about it?

Caller: I did, but he's still the same. Sometimes we have a date for dinner or for a movie and, well, he forgets and he doesn't come.

Radio: You're kidding!

Caller: No. I'm serious. He's always making excuses. One time he had to help his mother. One time his car didn't work. One time he said he had an accident. I don't know what to do. Maybe he has another girlfriend. What should I do?

Radio: Well, I think you should talk to Jim again. Maybe he's worried about something. In any case, communication is the best answer to your problem. If he can't talk to you or if he won't talk to you, then maybe he isn't the man for you.

Caller: Yes, I guess you're right. Well, thank you.

Radio: Thank you for calling "Help Line." . . . Hello. This is "Help Line." How can I help you?

Lesson 1, exercise 3, p. 112

Listen and complete this conversation.

Isabel: Mom, do I really have to help Dad?

Olga: Yes, you do. He wants to clean the garage, and he needs your help.

Isabel: Did you have to help your parents when you were my age?

Olga: Yes. As a matter of fact, I had to work in your grandfather's store.

Isabel: When did you have to work?

Olga: I had to help him on the weekends and after school.

Isabel: What did you have to do?

Olga: I cleaned around the store, and when it was very busy I had to help the customers.

Isabel: What else did you have to do?

Olga: Sometimes I had to cook dinner and clean the house.

Isabel: Why did you have to do that?

Olga: Because your grandmother wasn't well, and she couldn't do it.

Lesson 2, exercise 4, p. 116

Tony is calling his neighbor, Jeff. Listen and choose the correct answers.

Tony: Hi. Jeff? This is Tony. Listen, we're having a party for one of my classmates, and we don't have enough dishes. Have you got any plates?

Jeff: Sure. How many do you need?

Tony: Four. Have you got any cups and saucers? I need nine.

Jeff: I've only got four, but you can use them.

Tony: OK. And how about knives and forks?

Jeff: I've got a lot of them. How many do you want?

Tony: Eleven knives and thirteen forks.

Jeff: OK. Anything else?

Tony: Have you got any napkins?

Jeff: Gee, let's see. I think I have some paper napkins . . . No, sorry, I haven't got any.

Tony: That's OK. I'll be right over for the other things.

Lesson 3, exercise 2, p. 118

Listen to this conversation and write the woman's questions.

Woman: You're going to take the next English course, aren't you?

Man: Yes, I think so.

Woman: What are you doing during school break?

Man: I'm going to Miami. I'm leaving on Saturday.

Woman: What are you going to do there?

Man: I'm going to visit friends. We'll probably just go to the beach and relax.

Woman: That sounds good. When will you be back?

Man: In a week.

Woman: Will you send me a postcard?

Man: Sure.

Woman: You won't forget, will you?

Man: Of course not.